# 21 Days to
# a *Better*
# Quiet Time
# with God

## Books in the 21-Day Series

Proven Plan
for Beginning
New Habits

# 21 Days to a *Better* Quiet Time with God

## Timothy Jones

### *Series Editor*
### Dan Benson

ZondervanPublishingHouse
*Grand Rapids, Michigan*

*A Division of HarperCollinsPublishers*

98 99 00 01 02 03 04 /❖ DC/ 10 9 8 7 6 5 4 3 2 1

# BIOGRAPHICAL NOTE

Timothy Jones is a freelance writer, editor, and speaker. His specialty is prayer and the spiritual life. Until recently he was managing editor for Moorings, a Nashville-based division of the Ballantine Publishing Group. For almost six years before joining Moorings, Timothy was an editor at *Christianity Today* magazine. For eight years before that he was a pastor. He graduated with a master's degree from Princeton Theological Seminary in 1979. His other books include *The Art of Prayer, Celebration of Angels* (with over 100,000 copies in print), and *The Saints Among Us* coauthored with pollster George Gallup Jr. He lives in the Nashville, Tennessee, area with his wife, Jill, and three children.

# CONTENTS

# PREFACE

Do you long to find new richness for your devotional times?

You're not alone.

Everybody's talking about the spiritual life these days, it seems. Nine out of ten Americans say they pray, according to polls. Words like *spirituality* and *prayer* excite unprecedented interest, even outside the church. And within the church, leaders report an unheard-of interest in learning how to pray. Some observers call it a "quiet revolution."

Even so, probably no area of the Christian life produces more resolutions—and greater guilt—than our devotional habits. "I know I should pray and have regular quiet times," a friend of mine once confessed, "and I want to. But it's a struggle." After all, who of us hasn't determined to spend more time in God's presence only to experience disappointment? We'd like to pray more. We'd love to make room for quiet in a noisy life. And we'd gladly spend more time reading the Bible. But for all our attempts, we tend toward cycles of great plans and fallen hopes, feast and famine. Our progress comes in spurts at best. It all may lead to what I call a devotional guilt complex.

I've seen it firsthand. And I've seen it in myself. For years I've had a special passion for the subject. The one class my seminary offered on spiritual life was not enough; I have in the almost twenty years since pursued the topic vigorously. My shelves groan with the scores of books I've collected on prayer. When I was a pastor, I preached and taught about spiritual life regularly. Now I give workshops on prayer. Through it all I have seen a recurring problem: When I teach about the devotional life to groups, or even just mention it to friends, I can sometimes imagine my listeners mentally rolling their eyes and thinking, *If he only knew the real me. . . .* We know God commands us to spend time with him. We've seen God use our prayers in mighty ways, yet our devotions often get lost in the "muchness" and "manyness" of daily life. "I feel like some-body has set up some kind of standard I've got to live up to," a friend admitted. "And I rarely do." You live with a weight of unmet (and sometimes unrealistic) expectations. Mortgage payments, squirmy kids, demanding bosses, and sometimes your own lukewarm feelings conspire against your best intentions. A vital, truly transforming devotional life seems always just out of reach. And when you *do* manage to find time for devotions, the joy doesn't last for long. You fall into a rut. You ask yourself, *Can't I find a better way?*

## I HAVE GOOD NEWS: YOU *CAN!*

What you are about to read will show you how to cultivate quiet times you can look forward to. It will help you build a devotional life that feels less like a duty, more like a delight; not just a routine but a time for relating to God in joyous freedom. You can shed the false guilt and fears that hold you back. No longer need you feel resigned to simply going through the motions. Times consciously spent in the presence of God—whether morning or evening, whether for an hour or a few quick minutes—can become some of the most significant times of your day. I know that change can happen because it is happening in me. It has happened in scores of people I know—people I have learned from. You can discover simple yet profoundly helpful ways to have richer quiet times.

Think of what follows as a gently unfolding, day-by-day adventure of discovery. You will learn, to highlight just a few examples, how to:

- Start simply, without confusing, joy-killing regimens.
- Approach God expectantly, not fearfully or grudgingly.
- Establish a balanced devotional diet.
- Read the Bible for all it's worth, letting God speak to your daily life.
- Let others' prayers jump-start yours.
- Make friends with silence, a quiet that is far more than the absence of sound.
- Listen to God's still, small voice.
- Dip into the devotional classics (treasures the church has almost forgotten).
- Draw near to God through music.
- Experiment with new approaches, becoming acquainted with a variety you perhaps never knew existed.
- Make plans for regular quiet times—realistic plans that *work*.

## WELCOME TO THE 21-DAY EXPERIENCE!

It takes time to ingrain new patterns. People who study human behavior say it takes twenty-one days for a practice to become a habit. But patterning new ways to spend time in God's presence may never have been so enjoyable! You are about to embark on more than a day-by-day process. You are about to embark on a spiritual adventure. Over the next twenty-one days you will be challenged to try new approaches. You may be nudged you out of stale ways of thinking. But your quiet times will be injected with new life, new confidence. A friend of mine says that a person can do just about anything new for three weeks. After that, it begins to feel natural. Give it a try!

Don't worry about doing it all "just right." This is about relationship more than performance. There is plenty of room for fresh starts if you stumble. Don't feel that you have to follow the twenty-one-day format slavishly. Feel free to concentrate on God and his goodness to you, not on punching a devotional time clock or achieving heroic feats.

And while you should approach all this without a heavy weight of expectations for your performance, I believe great things are about to happen for you. "Pray . . . ," Paul the apostle wrote long ago, "on all occasions with all kinds of prayers and requests" (Eph. 6:18). Paul knew that prayer can take place in all kinds of seasons and circumstances, and with varied means and patterns. You are about to encounter some of the breadth and depth of what Paul called "all kinds of prayers." Even in twenty-one days you won't exhaust all the potential for growth. That will take a lifetime! But you can start. And your quiet times—and your everyday life—will be the better for it.

## Start Simply

*Come as you are and begin wherever you are.*

Do you sometimes feel there can be more to your prayer and Bible study times than you experience now? Chances are you can identify with at least one of the people I'm about to describe, all of whom long to find a more satisfying devotional life.

Picture with me: Tom, a lanky thirty-something executive who stands out in most crowds. But it's not his height that makes him so obvious at the Southern California company where he works. His wit and leadership skills make him a magnet for things that need fixing at the office. He has proven himself so valuable to his company, in fact, that he usually feels snowed under by the tasks his bosses constantly assign him. And work isn't the only problem. Leaders at Tom's suburban church long ago discovered his communication gifts and infectious good humor. They approach him all the time with projects and "ministry opportunities." On top of it all, Tom keenly cares about his family—a wife with a job of her own and two delightfully active school-age children. "I like what I'm doing," he once confessed, "but how can I move through this time without neglecting my soul? How can I pay more attention to my spiritual side when I'm so busy?"

Margaret, a Midwesterner just out of college, faces a different dilemma. As a doctor's receptionist, she stays busy enough, but it's not her *schedule* that makes having a regular devotional time hard. It's not knowing what to do when she does sit down. She attends worship faithfully, even goes to Bible study classes, but questions still persist when she thinks about that period every day where she tries to pray and read the Bible. "How do I hear God's voice?" she once wondered out loud. "What am I supposed to say when I pray? And how do I know if I'm doing it 'right'?" Sometimes she finds it easier not to try, and she sleeps in.

Or there's Bill, a retired school administrator, who wrestles with still another obstacle. He knows his Bible well; he estimates he's taught his popular New Testament 101 Sunday school class to hundreds of attentive adults. He's lost count of the theology books he's read and collected over the years. But sometimes he feels vaguely restless over how *ordinary* his prayer times seem. At conferences he hears speakers relate stories of prayer times charged with God's presence, but when he sits down to pray at night before he turns out his bedside light, he feels dry, uninspired. He goes through his list of people needing prayer, even reads from the Psalms. But he can't escape the nagging feeling that he is missing something.

Tom and Margaret and Bill all embody common struggles. Your issue may be similar or a bit different. But whatever keeps your times with God from being all you'd like, one bit of beginning wisdom applies universally: It's best to start simply.

Some people find that advice the best news they've heard in a long time. After years of feeling that they had to prove something to God, after a life of feeling guilty for not daily setting their alarms for 5:00 A.M. prayer; after finally realizing that their beloved and saintly aunt's prayer "method" didn't really fit, they finally are free to stand before God without a burden of guilt.

Rather than assume that the devotional life must be complicated, reserved for saints or monks, consider these three handles for starting simply:

## 1. BEGIN WHERE YOU ARE

No other conviction has done more to free me. I am realizing that I need not have everything put together "just so" to pray. I come as I am. How could any of us approach time with God in any other way?

God is not as interested in your fine phrases or in your meeting him punctually every day as he is in *you*. This is not a business proposition or a science experiment. We are not talking about legal contracts. Growth comes not with charts and maps but with a simple desire for God. Quiet times hinge on relationship, not on procedure.

My friend Kevin, perhaps as faithful in seeking God as anyone I know, gives this advice: "Don't 'guilt yourself.' Set realistic goals. Build your times spent in God's presence around who you are."

Starting where you are may mean several things. Perhaps you need to sense a new freedom in your quiet times. You can come to your quiet times without concern for flowery language. Your prayers need not mimic those of your favorite writer or the members of your Sunday school class. Nor should you ever feel that you must, as a friend of mine once said, use big theological words in the hope that God will then (and only then) hear. God has made you for himself; learning to talk to God is not like mastering a foreign language. If it helps, picture God, as someone I know once did, as a friend sitting in a chair near you. Converse as naturally with God as you would with a friend. After all, God can hear your faintest whisper and quietest utterance. Talking to God as a friend can help you relax. Time with God can take on a refreshing familiarity. In more than one place in the New Testament we are encouraged to call God *Abba,* an ancient, affectionate term for father much like our name *Daddy.*

The timing for your conversations with God need not be rigid or intricate. It has taken me some time to learn this. I once met a woman who decided one day to make a commitment to a one-hour quiet time every day. She made it an irrevocable decision and suggested, as she told her story, that perhaps all Christians should do the same. My conscience was pricked by her resolve. I was moved by her faith, just as I was made uncomfortably aware of how unheroic my devotional life was.

But by this time in my Christian life I knew that I needed more than new resolutions. Instead of just trying harder, I began to pray *about my praying.* I expressed to God my frustrated longings, my sense of failure over trying to be more disciplined. I came as I *was.*

Something surprising happened: Rather than condemnation, I felt God's gentle invitation to come and continue to come to him—whenever I could, however I could. I was drawn into the presence of One who had the power to keep me close, to do what I could not do on my own. Prayer is for dummies, sinners, and everyday people who constantly mess up and embarrass themselves. God honors our efforts, wherever we are.

---

Try this: As you begin your quiet time today, "introduce" yourself to God. Tell God whatever is on your mind. Don't waste any energy wondering if you are saying the right things or feeling "spiritual" thoughts. Feel free to say, "God, this is who I am. This is what I want." Decide to enjoy being with God.

## 2. DON'T TRY SO HARD THAT YOUR QUIET TIME BECOMES A BURDEN

It is true that God is not to be trifled with, that devotion sometimes requires great discipline, that prayer is urgent business. And yes, Paul tells us to "devote" ourselves to prayer (Col. 4:2). He even tells us in 1 Thessalonians 5:17 to "pray continually"— or, as some translations have, "without ceasing." But that does not mean you must constantly grit your teeth to make something "happen." Let your times before God have an unstrained simplicity. The goal is encountering God, not showing off or proving something. We pray, just as we live, to glorify God and enjoy him forever, as the old Presbyterian catechism reminds us. We should not think of what some call the spiritual disciplines "as some dull drudgery aimed at exterminating laughter from the face of the earth," says writer Richard Foster. "Joy is the keynote of the Disciplines. . . . Singing, dancing, even shouting characterize the Disciplines of the spiritual life."[1]

Your time with God can flourish with wonderful freedom and variety. You can seek God in the mornings, over your lunch break, or while on an evening stroll around the block. Once a wise spiritual mentor encouraged me to find "pools of prime time" in each week. If I couldn't pray an hour every morning, perhaps I could find an afternoon during a weekend to devote to prayer. Perhaps I could sometimes take a long lunch break and walk a wooded park trail to be alone with God. I could relax about it all.

What actually happens in these invaluable times may vary, too. You may be drawn to keeping lists of people who urgently need prayers, filling most of your time with intercession. Or you may, like a friend of mine, sometimes find yourself spending almost all your quiet time immersed in the Bible, awed by the truths that continue to unfold there. I once met a couple who enjoyed singing their prayers through hymns and praise choruses. You may log your prayers and insights faithfully in a journal. Some pray best when they first awaken, others after the kids are out the door to catch the school bus. I have some of my richest prayer times as I jog in the early morning hours. Perhaps your half-hour commute to work provides your only consistent place of quiet. I'll say more about these options later, but for now know that my approach is not going to be to stifle your experimenting. Quiet times do not unfold along a rigid outline.

You may find yourself drawn to different kinds of prayer at different times of your life. Not so long ago, I decided that for one day I needed to devote every impulse to prayers of praise and thanksgiving. A whole day of quietly uttered thanks! I don't feel called to do that all the time, of course, but what a glorious day that was!

A creative, spontaneous spirit can serve you well in your quest for more satisfying quiet times. Don't feel that prayer must follow a rigid pattern or that what you do today must dictate what you do tomorrow. *You* are important in this enterprise, too. God wants this time to be more than an obligation; he wants it to be a source of rest, refreshment, and joy.

---

Try this: Pause for a moment to reflect on James 4:8, which says, "Draw near to God and He will draw near to you"(NASB). How might that promise help you relax as you come to God?

## 3. GIVE YOURSELF TIME TO DEEPEN AND GROW

Some aspects of the devotional life take practice just to get the hang of them. You have to trust what someone has called the "slow work of God." You celebrate the small steps forward. When you fall back or fail, tell God about it, receive his forgiveness, and move ahead.

I grew up in a churchgoing family in southern California. My parents had my brother and me "say grace" aloud every time we gathered around the supper table. I majored in religious studies in college, and I was graduated almost two decades ago from Princeton Theological Seminary. I have read many books and articles on prayer—have even written a few. And I have managed most days, between stumbling out of bed and downing my breakfast, to fit in time for morning prayers. But I realize again and again how far I am from plumbing the depths of God. God patiently carries me along. We begin and then begin again. There will always be room to grow.

What you are about in your quiet times should have more the feel of ongoing adventure than static obligation. Ups and downs will come, surely, but because you are not in this alone, because God *invites* us to pray, you can set aside the fear. Let go of that temptation to turn this into one more competitive "project." You are about to be liberated to *grow,* not to strive. "He who began a good work in you," Paul reminded the church at Philippi, "will carry it on to completion" (Phil. 1:6). God will take our simple beginnings and lead us to a better place.

---

Try this: Take a few moments to talk to God, telling him you are ready to begin, or to begin again, and that you want to see your quiet times grow in richness and meaning.

## LESSON OF THE DAY

*Come as you are and begin
wherever you are.*

# DAY 2

## Approach God Confidently

*Come to your quiet time with anticipation.*

A friend who regularly leads prayer workshops often begins her teaching with a question: "Do you feel that you pray enough—that you are satisfied with your devotional life? If so, raise your hand." The response from attendees, she told me, never varies: "*Nobody* raises a hand."

Can we never feel content and confident about our devotional lives? Will there always be some standard—spoken or unspoken—that seems just out of reach?

I want to set you at ease. Your devotional life need not leave you feeling constantly defeated. No matter how "undisciplined" you have been, no matter how many erratic starts you've made, no matter how "green" you feel in your Christian experience, I want to help free you from the guilt of never "making it."

I am going to do so, however, in a way that may surprise you. I'm not going to counsel that you simply content yourself with halfhearted efforts. Instead, I want to reframe the issue altogether. I want you to believe that no matter what devotions have meant to you in the past, you can begin your quiet time today with confidence. For what happens in that time of prayer and Bible study will not hinge on some knack on your part or on your being wonderfully regular. It rests on something—Someone—else. With that insight in mind, three pointers will make the difference in how you approach your devotional time today.

## 1. COME CONFIDENTLY, BECAUSE PERFORMANCE IS NOT THE POINT

I once was struck by a junk mail offer that crossed by desk. It announced a book entitled *How to Do Everything Right*. Sample tips from the book's contents were intended to whet my appetite, like how to get off the phone without offending the talkative party on the other end, or how to get rid of impossible stains. But the real clincher was the bold caption: "421 inside ways to live better, smarter, longer, safer—*and* richer—in uncertain times when you need to be an expert on *everything*."

Perhaps you labor under a subtle pressure to do everything "right" when it comes to your quiet time. Let me set you at ease. The most appropriate attitude is not "rightness" but dependence. Not haughtiness, but humility. Remember Jesus' story of the Prodigal Son (Luke 15:11–32)? The wayward son was not welcomed because of his goodness. He came in humility and trust, knowing he had to rely on another's gracious forgiveness.

In your quiet time, the point is not achievement. We need not hold back from coming to God till we think we are finally doing it all "right." To borrow the Nike advertising slogan, we tell ourselves, "Stop worrying about yourself, your words, your efforts. Just *do* it."

All this became supremely relevant to me one morning. Before leaving the house for a doctor's appointment, I realized I had a few spare moments. (Getting six-year-old Bekah out the door for kindergarten had precluded my normal quiet time.) My first thought was to sit down with my Bible. But then I saw my computer and remembered I was expecting some e-mail, so I turned on the computer. Yes, the message was there, but it was a mixture of good news and disappointment. I felt compelled to respond in some detail to the message. By the time I was done, I barely had time for breakfast. I rushed out the door and felt agitated, realizing I had missed an opportunity to spend a few moments in God's presence. I felt regret.

But then I realized, *here I am going to be in the car for a half hour on the way to the doctor's office.* I prayed for much of it. Then, once at the office, I had time in the waiting room to pull out my Bible and read and reflect. God received me with open arms. I needed to not let my guilt keep me from praying when I could. To top it off, that morning I soon turned my attention to the writings of Julian, a medieval Christian renowned for his writings about God's love. What did I read? "For as the body is clothed in cloth and the flesh in skin and the bones in the flesh and the heart in the torso, so are we, soul and body, clothed and enclosed in the goodness of God. Indeed, more truly, for they all vanish and waste away. The goodness of God is always whole and nearer to us, without any comparison."[1]

---

Try this: Reflect on how your attitudes toward your quiet time sometimes make you fall into a performance trap. Remind yourself that nothing in yourself need hold you back.

Which leads to the second point.

## 2. COME CONFIDENTLY BECAUSE OF WHO GOD IS

Humility by itself won't get you far. You also need a right understanding of God. Nothing will do more to shape your expectation and experience of your time with God.

At a library recently I saw a book about prayer with an interesting title: *Praying: How, Where, When, Why.* I thought, *Not a bad title.* The book looked quite good; people should know what to pray for, where to do it, and how. But something critical had been left off the title: *Who!* More than anything else, we need to consider the God we talk to. Because the only thing that makes prayer anything is God.

Take the focus off yourself. Put the focus on the God of the universe and everything changes. Suddenly your limits fall away. Your fears melt. You realize that what happens in prayer has to do most of all with God's tenderness and power.

Not long ago I was struggling with something I was writing about the spiritual life. I was searching for the right angle, but it wasn't coming together. Then my wife asked me a telling question: "I don't really know why you pray. Why do you care so much about it? That's not always clear." And I realized something I sometimes take for granted, something I don't always articulate to others or even to myself: I come to God because I have an expectation that *something significant* will happen. Of course, I pray because disciples are commanded to pray. I pray because prayer is a discipline and obligation of the Christian life. But what really makes me pray is not so much willpower as expectation:

- I expect to meet God.
- I expect that God will take what I ask for into account.
- I expect that God will be able to do something about what I say.

Realizing all this has made me excited about my devotional times in a way I hadn't been for some time. Why do I do it? Because there, behind my listening, my Bible reading, even my sometimes distracted praying, operates the very power and goodness and trustworthiness of God.

Think about how we almost always start our prayers, with an address—"Dear God ..." or "Heavenly Father ..." In the Lord's Prayer in Matthew 6, Jesus encourages us to start with "Our Father in heaven." In doing so, we make a statement about God and God's power, God's character. We set the tone for what happens. Take that one step further: Before you get going very far in your quiet time today, think about the God you address. Ask yourself not "How do I spend this time?" Begin with the question, "With whom am I spending this time?"

If you do, you will find yourself thinking about the wonder of God. You will begin to remember some of the things the Bible says about God—that he is wise, limitless, creative, mighty, eternal, and resourceful. Begin your devotional times with thinking about the unfathomable greatness of God, and prayer will become not just a duty but a delight.

---

Try this: Reflect on the following passages as you think about today's quiet time. Ask yourself how they can fill you with new confidence about the God you approach.

> [God] alone is my rock and my salvation;
>     he is my fortress, I will never be shaken.
> (Ps. 62:2)

> The LORD is faithful to all his promises. . . .
> The LORD is righteous in all his ways
>     and loving toward all he has made.
> The LORD is near to all who call on him,
>     to all who call on him in truth.
> (Ps. 145:13, 17–18)

> Oh, the depth of the riches of the wisdom and knowledge of God! . . . "Who has known the mind of the Lord? Or who has been his counselor?" "Who has ever given to God, that

God should repay him?" For from him and through him and to him are all things. To him be the glory forever! Amen.

(Rom. 11:33–36)

### 3. COME TO GOD CONFIDENTLY BECAUSE OF HOW GOD RESPONDS

This morning, while I was out jogging, I took along a small card with a verse from the Psalms I'm memorizing. "In the morning, O LORD," it read, "you hear my voice; in the morning I lay my requests before you and wait in *expectation*." God not only *exists* in goodness and love, he also *acts* and *responds* that way. God puts his ear down to our heart's whispered desires. His loving, inviting character makes all the difference.

After all, it is one thing to talk about a God of limitless power. But while might and vastness might impress us, even fascinate us, they won't necessarily *invite* us. Surely David the Psalmist had this in mind when he penned, "Two things have I heard: that you, O God, are strong, and that you, O Lord, are loving" (Ps. 62:11–12). The God who is *able* to help cares enough that he *wants* to help. He promises to get involved.

Jesus painted a striking picture to make sure we realize that. "Which of you fathers," he once asked a crowd, "if your son asks for a fish, will give him a snake instead? Or if he asks for an egg, will give him a scorpion? If you then, though you are evil, know how to give good gifts to your children, how much more will your Father in heaven give the Holy Spirit to those who ask him!" (Luke 11:11–13).

Christianity has always taught grace. A relationship with God is something we receive, not achieve. And just as our salvation begins with letting go of all of the accomplishments we think make us presentable to God, so does our growth in our quiet times. Other religions say we pray to get through to God. But Jesus demonstrated that the point is not that we find God, but that *he* has found *us*. *Salvation*, the Bible's word for Christ's redemption and our rescue from self and sin, is not our doing, but God's. We accept what God has done. That is what the coming of Jesus means. That is the good news of Christianity. That is the good news about your quiet time.

"How wonderful and beyond knowing, O God," *The Book of Common Prayer* recites, "is your mercy and loving kindness to us, that to redeem a slave, you gave a Son." A friend of mine puts it even more simply: Because of what Christ did, I'm unrejectable. I may stumble, I may not pray just right, but God still receives me.

Perhaps you tend to come to God out of conscience instead of confidence. Today approach God with the eager expectation that he will be there—listening, helping, and lending his hand.

***

Try this: Today make your approach not one of grudging duty but of confidence that in prayer you will meet God himself, that when you pray he will be there—for you.

## LESSON OF THE DAY

*Come to your quiet time with anticipation.*

# Establish a Balanced Devotional Diet

*Your quiet times need never get stuck or static.*

I*'m in a devotional rut.* That's how I felt one morning when I sat down for my quiet time. I had been following a list of people to pray for and reading the Bible. But something was lacking. I knew that mystics' raptures do not always attend quiet times. But I sensed that this time I needed to do more than clench my teeth and stick to it. No, I realized that my devotions were getting anemic. I soon saw how I had been neglecting to praise God and simply enjoy his presence. My devotional time turned a corner when I did.

Perhaps you can identify. You sit down but nothing much seems to happen. Or maybe you haven't yet encountered a dry season; you just want to make sure your devotional times are as rich as possible. I want to encourage your good intentions. Even if you are too new to this habit to have formed any ruts, you will, sometime in the future, find yourself ready for more than the "same old same old." Establishing a balanced prayer diet is an important step in making your devotional times all they can be.

And rest assured: Your quiet time does not have to be a dull, monochrome custom. You don't have to do this all by rote. You don't have to slavishly follow another's scheme. Devotion is a many-splendored thing. Just as no two people are alike, no two people must spend time with God in precisely the same way. Don't feel you must adopt some sonorous, stained-glass tone in your praying just because your pastor from childhood did. Don't try to clone your aunt's quiet time "method."

Of course, some people don't feel such freedom. Prayer *has* to be at 6:00 A.M. (or some other predetermined, obviously "holy" time). They won't consider letting in laughter or music (too distracting). And Bible reading? The more organized and weighty, the better, they seem to think. Stiff formality is the hallmark of it all. But such life-squelching somberness denies some fundamental, foundational truths about prayer.

Later we'll look at the varied forms and patterns your quiet times can take, but for now you can move toward a balanced devotional life by attending to the three basic movements of our relationship with God. They can make a difference in today's quiet time—and those of the months and years to come.

## 1. ENCOUNTER

Often the first act of devotion is to simply be present. We "show up." And not just physically. We turn our attention gently toward the God we expect to meet. We wait in expectancy for him to make his loving presence known. Devotion is first and foremost a *meeting* between Creator and creature. Father and child. Lover and beloved. So we come with more than concern about what we need to say or do. We approach our devotions with our *selves,* not just our requests. "Come near to God," James 4:8 tells us, "and he will come near to you." "Seek the

LORD while he may be found; call on him while he is near," Isaiah the prophet invited (Isa. 55:6).

While this is simple, it is not always easy. The countless details of normal life may crowd out your awareness of God. While everyday concerns belong in your praying, sometimes they can also conspire against your seeking and receiving God. When my wife, Jill, and I come home after a busy day at our offices, we have to leave behind the clamor and clutter before we can really be present; so also you and I may come to God distracted, needing to gather our focus. C. S. Lewis once wrote that the moment you wake up each morning, "All your wishes and hopes for the day rush at you like wild animals. And the first job each morning consists simply in shoving them all back; in listening to that other voice, taking that other point of view, letting that other, larger, stronger, quiet life come flowing in."[1] When we shed the distractions, God comes and blesses us. And we lovingly gaze back. We rest in the goodness of a God who loves us. But it all requires intention.

There is another side, too. We don't spoil our times with God with a breathless concern to pay attention. Steve Brown tells of a friend who, after a few years away from God, started praying again. "I asked her," Steve writes, "about her prayers, expecting to hear a description of how she had spent hours repenting, confessing, adoring, praising, and petitioning God. She said, 'Steve, you aren't going to think it is much of a prayer. I just say to him before I go to sleep, 'Good night, Jesus.'"[2] The desire to meet God is what really counts, not perfect concentration.

This can give our praying wonderful freedom. Think of an intimate relationship in your life: with a child, with a spouse, with a cherished friend. If it is healthy, there are times in your relating that you simply enjoy being together. Your coming with a calendar in hand and a list of "discussion items" would spoil a precious moment. Chatter for the sake of filling the spaces would stifle closeness.

The fact that devotion is about relationship has other freeing outcomes. You can be creative about the when and where you meet God, for example. There's a woman I know who finds she prays best in her customary two-hour wide-awake period in the middle of the night. I would hesitate to prescribe that pattern to anyone, but I don't doubt that God makes his presence vividly real to her. I sometimes have at least a portion of my quiet time while I take my morning jog in the neighborhood. My wife, on the other hand, has trouble praying while walking or driving. She needs a quiet spot and uninterrupted time. That's okay, too. You can listen for God's voice in the morning, during a lunch break, or cruising a supermarket aisle. You may have quiet time inside or outside. You can pray quietly or sing. You can read the Bible book by book or topic by topic. A chapter a day is a good goal for many people, but some mornings one verse may speak volumes. Wondering about posture? You can sit, lie, or walk during your devotions (more on that later). What you discuss with God, the ways you reflect on your life, and the insights you glean from Scripture don't have to be force-fit into someone's mold. And the less you feel compelled to do so, the more likely you are to develop, with the Lord's help, a well-balanced approach.

Because prayer is an encounter with a loving God, not a cosmic grouch, you don't have to be overly serious. Don't think there must be a dull, routine regularity for it to count. We come not with a slave's obligation to a harsh master but with a child's delight in running to her father. Remember David, dancing before the Lord "with all his might" as the ark of the Lord was taken into Jerusalem. Remember how when the Lord rescued the Israelites from Egyptian bondage, Miriam picked up a tambourine and sang,

> Sing to the LORD,
>     for he is highly exalted.
> The horse and its rider
>     he has hurled into the sea (Ex. 15:21).

These biblical mentors in prayer discovered the freedom of loving encounter. They found that we can meet the God whom our hearts always are longing for. God is as eager to be close to us as we are to approach him—usually more so—and he greets us with joy.

––––––––––

Try this: Take five minutes to simply become aware that God is close. Don't worry about saying anything or "accomplishing" anything. Just become aware of God.

## 2. TALK

Spend time with anyone and soon you naturally, inevitably find yourself talking. For human beings, few things come more naturally than vocalizing what we think and feel. It's that way from birth. People who study language (and any parent) will tell you that infants begin to pick up words without prodding or pushing, seemingly automatically, without vocabulary drills and other techniques of formal training. Talking seems to be built into our genes. And talking, therefore, forms a vital part of any balanced devotional life. Words, for all their limitations, can serve us wonderfully.

But while the impulse to talk is constantly there, the facility may not be. We sometimes hesitate because we think we don't know what to say. We feel at a loss for words. We fear there is some "right" way to pray, that missing that will leave our prayers unheard and unanswered. We may even feel embarrassed when we try. Or we become troubled when we don't "feel" words pouring out in an unbroken stream.

But I have good news. That we *want* to talk to God in our quiet times suggests that we can. And that words can come naturally. God has built in us a longing and hunger that drives us to address him. As for the words themselves, often simpler is better. The eloquence God most cares about is one of the heart, not the lips. Stuttering prayers born of humble, heartfelt longing mean more than a dictionary's worth of fine words.

Whatever you do, keep praying. God likes to hear us talk.

Try this: Experiment with offering God simple words of devotion. See your devotional time as a conversation in which you can feel free to express whatever is on your mind.

## 3. LISTEN

After I have shared with God what is on my mind, I often forget to "hang around" for a response. But often the most significant portions of my devotional times unfold when I stop talking. Waiting in the Lord's presence often yields great blessing, personal insight, or much-needed direction for an important decision. Sometimes God reminds me of his immeasurable greatness and disarming love. God may remind me how carefully he cares for me, especially significant when I'm anxious about something.

But how do you listen—and know it's really God? How does God make himself and his will known? My oldest son is in the throes of deciding what college to go to next year or even if he should wait a year. "I'm afraid," Abram told me today, "that I will pray for God's guidance but won't hear anything." The whole issue of listening troubles many Christians. Many feel a burden of pressure to somehow hear some grand revelation. And who of us doesn't occasionally worry that we will miss critical guidance?

A person could write a whole book on how to listen to God (as many have). But let me assure you that what you do right now can be wonderfully simple. The important thing is to cultivate an attitude of openness. We simply do our part. We open the ears of our heart. We tell God we want to be faithful. "You will seek me and find me when you seek me with all your heart," the Lord said through Jeremiah (29:13).

One of my favorite Old Testament passages suggests a practical way to do this. When the Lord began calling young Samuel the prophet, the boy did not realize it was God. He ran to Eli, his guardian and the temple priest, mistakenly thinking he was hearing Eli's voice. Eli finally told the puzzled youth, "Go and lie down, and if [God] calls you, say, 'Speak, LORD, for your servant is listening'" (1 Sam. 3:9). Samuel did, and the Lord spoke.

We can say such prayers expectantly. God is not a miser with his guidance. He has at his disposal a host of means to get through to us. He speaks through his revealed will in Scripture and through the counsel of wise friends. He often speaks through a godly minister and through a spiritually committed spouse or parent. He may even speak directly through a still, small voice. Such a conviction frees us to listen without forcing and to go about our daily lives confident God will communicate.

---

Try this: Take Samuel's prayer in 1 Samuel 3:9–10 ("Speak, LORD, for your servant is listening") and make it your own. As you get up from your quiet time, keep it on your lips and in your heart.

## LESSON OF THE DAY

*Your quiet times need never get stuck or static.*

# Read Scripture for All It's Worth (Part 1)

*Read the Bible not only for information but for personal transformation.*

Recently I went through a time when my Bible reading seemed flat. God still spoke through those morning devotions, deepening my faith in ways I could only glimpse. And when crisis or fear drove me to the Bible, I never came away without some encouragement. But in the long haul, something seemed missing. I tried daily plans—with assigned blocks of the Bible to read each day—but when I fell behind, as I frequently did, I ended up more frustrated than before. Other times I would pick a book of the Bible to read, chapter by chapter, verse by verse, but the whole enterprise was vaguely unsatisfying.

If you are like me, you would love to bring new depth to an activity that sometimes seems hit-or-miss. Perhaps you wonder if it's possible to be diligent in Bible reading without dampening spontaneity and joy. Or perhaps regular Bible reading has you a bit intimidated; you simply need gentle coaching and reassurance. Wherever you find yourself, I suspect you are eager for a way of Bible reading that helps you listen to God. You want to let the Word within the words address your daily life. You don't want to miss any of God's revealed riches.

I have been helped in this through an ancient Christian practice with a musty-sounding name—*lectio divina* (Latin for spiritual, or divine, reading). I am all for reading through whole books of the Bible and taking in large amounts of Scripture. But this way of "spiritual reading" stresses soaking in truth, not accumulating concepts; reflecting on what God might be saying, not rushing through. I find it a meaningful way to read the Bible for all it's worth. To help me remember the steps of spiritual reading, I lay them out with four *r*'s, two of which we will explore today, and two tomorrow.

## 1. READ

This first step is disarmingly simple. But reading devotionally is not like other kinds of reading; we don't approach the Bible as we would a manual or magazine. We read devotionally not just to be *in*formed but also *trans*formed. The goal is digesting truth. Nor do we come to Scripture as we would an escapist novel; we are not in this for entertainment as much as encounter. We want to hear God. We want to learn and grow and make ourselves available to God's guidance. We resist the temptation to "get finished," to keep looking ahead to see how much is left in the chapter or book. We aim at depth, not just breadth. We remember fourth-century preacher John Chrysostom's words, "It is not possible ever to exhaust the mind of Scripture. It is a well that has no bottom."

This desire to go deep means approaching the Bible in a certain way.

In your reading, for example, you may need to slow down. We are not just filling a mental hard drive; we are seeking wisdom that touches our hearts. We chew on truth, not gulp it down. So we may need a more leisurely, spacious approach to the Bible. Indeed, I find it important to begin my reading by *not* reading. I take a deep breath, settle into a comfortable position, and ask that God bless my time, that his written word become a living word. I recall that I am not trying to "master" the passage as much as to surrender to what God may want to tell me through it. Then I open my Bible, usually to where I left off the day before, and cover a section of Scripture that I can read in a reasonable amount of time, usually a few verses or perhaps a short chapter.

I don't worry so much about getting through a certain volume of verses as much as letting a verse or phrase or word get through to *me*. I may read the passage more than once—sometimes it takes lingering until deeper meanings sink in. I may not get terribly far, but I try to go *deep*. "The intent," notes Tilden Edwards, "is not to get to the end of a passage, but to the bottom of it."[1]

I also find it helpful to read until something grabs my attention, until I sense that God is speaking through some verse or phrase. I try to read with an alert heart. I watch for an insight that seems to stand out as something I particularly need to hear.

Recently, for example, I've been making my way through Paul's letter to the Romans. The first day I read the book's first seven verses, alert to what I might hear. I ended up coming back to the first verse, where I read, "Paul, a servant of Christ Jesus, called to be an apostle and set apart for the gospel of God—the gospel he promised beforehand through his prophets in the Holy Scriptures." It was that word *called* that caught my eye. For in recent months I have been praying about my own calling. I have been trying to juggle my responsibilities as a writer, editor, husband, father, and church member. In what ways is God directing me? I observed from that word *called* how Paul did not just stumble into his work and pursuits; no, he felt summoned to what he did. I could not help but bring my concern to fulfill God's purposes for me and others to my reading that morning.

Then, during another day's reading, I was struck by Paul's writing in Romans 2:28–29 about not being a person of God "outwardly" but "inwardly." I let God catch my attention with a simple phrase. I might not have impressed anyone with my speed, but I took notice of an idea vital to my Christian life.

I once read of a woman who found great release in this notion of slowing down to go deeper. She had been using passages of Scripture to guide her prayer and devotional times, she told her small group. But it became a struggle. "I felt I ought to be making myself find new passages to pray with," she said. "[But] deep down I was more attracted to going back to some of the single verses of Scripture which made such an impression on me, and staying with them." So she contented herself with reading verses such as "Fear not, it is I," "Maranatha! Our Lord, come!" and "His banner over me is love." She found herself freed from the burden of having to "produce something new in prayer all the time."[2]

## 2. REFLECT

This next step, sometimes called "meditation" (see Ps. 1:2), has us prayerfully pausing to consider what we are reading and hearing. Someone has called this kind of reflection "thinking in the presence of God." It means that we, like Mary, "treasure up" and "ponder" what the Lord wants to tell us (Luke 2:19). "In our meditation," writes Dietrich Bonhoeffer, "we ponder the chosen text on the strength of the promise that it has something utterly personal to say to us for this day and for our Christian life, that it is not only God's Word for the Church, but also God's Word for us individually."[3] Our Western culture, which values action and busyness more than reflection, sometimes makes this difficult. But the rewards are immeasurable.

Say you have been struck by Jesus' words in the Gospel of John, "I am the true vine, and my Father is the gardener.... Remain in me, and I will remain in you" (John 15:1, 4). Here are deep things worth more than a cursory acknowledgment. How rich such a passage can be if we creatively, devotedly brood on what God stirs up within us!

And this is no merely sentimental process. Reflection involves our minds, hearts, wills, and souls. Reflecting on Scripture will have you reviewing, repeating, thinking, feeling, and praying. You will use your intellect as well as your spirit. You may, for example, want to learn more about the actual background of the passage. You might turn to study notes in your Bible that give you a better grasp of what the words signify. You would learn, as I did, that the image of the vine is often used in the Old Testament as a symbol of Israel. And "when this imagery is used, Israel is often shown as lacking in some way."[4] It is in that context, in our need, that we read that Jesus is "the true vine." We recall that we have no fruitfulness apart from him.

And don't stop with background research. Ask questions like these:

- What would God have me learn from this about himself?
- About myself?
- About how I live before him?

Allow such questions to help you, in the words of Joshua 1:8, not to "let this Book of the Law depart from your mouth; meditate on it day and night, so that you may be careful to do everything written in it." Read with your heart as well as your head. Rummage around in the depths of your being, open to the richness of God's truth, ready to let yourself be addressed. Come to the Bible as a meal to enjoy and absorb, not a fast-food selection.

And come with a soul open to transformation. "Always," counsels one spiritual writer, "read the Scriptures with a heart ready to repent."[5] Reflection allows us to go beyond mere information to life-reorienting insight.

This also means coming expectantly. God will not always speak through a thunderclap revelation, of course. God usually forms us slowly, steadily. But still we have the promise of Scripture that God will convey to us what we need to become Christlike. We *can* grow into what God wants us to be. God is not miserly with conveying his purposes to us through the Bible. He will graciously communicate and guide.

It is this expectancy that will keep our Bible reading fresh and life-giving. "All Scripture," wrote Paul, "is God-breathed and is useful for teaching, rebuking, correcting and training in righteousness, so that the man of God may be thoroughly equipped for every good work" (2 Tim. 3:16). Reflecting on it allows God's ancient truth to become as relevant as today's board meeting at the office, today's cranky toddler, today's need to grow more Christlike in a difficult relationship. As you ponder God's Word, a written word becomes a living word. As you read and reflect, you will find God speaking in ways you may have only dreamed about. God will not leave you lacking in good things from his Word.

And that will put you in a perfect position for tomorrow's next steps in reading the Bible for all it's worth.

---

Try this: Select a passage of Scripture (no more than a short chapter) and read it unhurriedly, prayerfully. You might consider Genesis 2, Psalm 1 or 23, or even a single verse like Isaiah 55:1 or John 3:16. As you begin, ask God to speak through it and to you. Reread it, looking for a word or phrase that particularly affects you. Then spend five minutes "thinking in the presence of God" about what that word or phrase meant to those who first heard it and, most important, what it can mean to you.

## LESSON OF THE DAY

*Read the Bible not only for information but also for personal transformation.*

# Read Scripture for All It's Worth (Part 2)

*Approach Bible reading as a conversation with God.*

As helpful as you may have found yesterday's two r's of approaching the Bible—reading and reflecting—you may sense that you've just begun to hear God. You feel your appetite whetted. Don't be surprised; those two steps set in motion a life-changing—and lifelong—conversation with God. Today we continue that conversation with two more r's—responding and receiving, which round out and deepen what we've been calling spiritual reading (*lectio divina*). Spiritual writer Dom Marmion once summed up what can happen:

> Read under the eye of God until your heart is touched, then give yourself up to love.[1]

For that to happen, you not only read and reflect, you:

## 3. RESPOND

Here you move beyond pondering the biblical passage to gathering up its truths in your praying. In reading and reflecting, you were intently listening for God's word; now you reply. You form an answer or ask prayerful questions. You keep the conversation going.

Many find this freeing. They realize that they can react to God's word and talk to him about it. This third stage, writes seminary professor Robert Mulholland, "is the pouring out of ourselves in response to God's address to us."[2] Think of it as interactive Bible learning. Responding to God by praying about what we are learning is not only polite, it works the insights into us "down deep." Any teacher will tell you that students absorb lessons more fully when they can discuss material and have a chance to ask questions. It is similar in our devotions: In our Bible reading we thank God for an insight revealed in our reading or ask help to see better what he is saying. Or through our praying we take what he shows us and we bring it into the scenes of our daily lives. We enlist what we read and hear to pray about our work, our relationships, ourselves.

You can also feel free to wrestle with what God seems to say, unafraid of offending him. "After struggling with the word that touched it," writes Macrina Wiederkehr, "my heart responds in many different ways. Sometimes it stands in awe, rejoicing. . . . Sometimes it weeps. Sometimes it sings. There are times it tenderly talks to God. At other times my heart screams out in anger. . . . Sometimes it kneels with outstretched arms. . . . Sometimes it simply yearns for God."[3] Regardless of the specific response, which will vary from passage to passage or from day to day, we express in honesty and faith what is going on in us. We carry on the dialogue of truth begun by God's revelation in Scripture. We make it our own.

You may remember how yesterday I spoke of spending time with Romans 2:28–29, where I read, "A man is not a Jew if he is only one outwardly, nor is circumcision merely outward and physical. No, a man is a Jew if he is one inwardly." I mentioned how I pondered what it meant to be (and to become) a person of God *inwardly*. But as I kept reading, I was struck by the short sentence that followed, also in verse 29: "Such a man's praise is not from men, but from God." *Here* was something I needed to pray about! I asked God to help me not seek approval from others, but from him. I recalled in my praying how my need for others' acceptance has often been an issue, how it sometimes undermines my courage, how it sometimes distracts my resolve to be faithful. As I went jogging even later that morning, I asked God to continue to make clear what it would mean for me to live for him in this way. "Lord," I prayed, "I want to be a person who lives for your praise, not the approval of others." I did more than think about what I had read; I plowed it into the soil of my day through prayer. There it could take root and grow, perhaps sometimes in unseen ways.

Here is how one man reflected on the story of Jesus' encounter with the Samaritan woman at the well in John 4, where Jesus talks about living water. As the man read and reflected, he said, "Gradually it came back to me that when I was a kid I used to mess about in a field near my home where there was a spring. I used to try to block it up with sods, but they soon washed away. [The spring] never froze in the winter. I thought I really needed to remember what springs are like if Jesus' words were going to get through to me." Then came his response:

> I prayed that [Jesus] would show me what this spring meant. I really imagined the spring I used to play with. I listened to it. I drank from it. I splashed in it and watched it come clear again in no time. When the spring had become real, I imagined it inside me instead of outside me. It had never occurred to me to do anything like this before! I really felt that spring welling up in me. I bet I spent ten minutes just getting used to this sense of something wonderful flowing deep down inside. Then I . . . talked with Jesus about whether it was true that he had

given me "a spring of water welling up to eternal life" that never stopped, or froze over, and that I couldn't foul up.[4]

This man's reading gave him new grist for his praying.

Try it! Make your praying a part of your Bible reading, and your Bible reading a part of your praying. Continue with yesterday's passage and keep the conversation with God alive as God speaks through it and as you listen and respond.

Then leave time for one more step, the fourth and final *r*:

## 4. RECEIVE

Whereas in reading, reflecting, and responding we play an active role, in *receiving,* activity quiets. We stand in a state of open readiness. We are not trying to tell God something, nor are we straining to hear God tell us anything. We simply rest in God's presence, in his goodness.

If you have read something powerful this day, pause in the reality of the Lord who is speaking to you. Don't rush to "apply" what you have heard, or chomp at the bit to act on it. In this final movement we truly become recipients. If you are like me, you may assume that whatever happens in your quiet times depends on your determination. You tense your hands and make things "happen." But in reality we are the ones being sought. "The Bible is alive," Martin Luther once said; "it speaks to me; it has feet, it runs after me; it has hands, it lays hold of me." In this stage of receiving, then, we let God and his Word lay hold of us in love and power. We allow ourselves to be addressed. We relax our hands and open them to whatever God has. And, as is proper in any relationship, we don't feel that we must always chatter back. We leave room for reverent refreshment from the Lord's presence. We sit in quiet communion. We soak in God's goodness.

In some ways I find it harder to describe or define this fourth and final stage of spiritual reading. And that is as it should be. God's ways of gently revealing himself and his love to us defy rigid explanations. They do not easily reduce themselves to facile steps or stages. All I know is that sometimes God brings to my insides a quiet, restful lightness. I know he is simply *here*.

My times of Bible reading do not always lead to this quiet state. I doubt if they will for you. So don't force anything. Some days you may be distracted enough that you do well to simply read and reflect. But more and more, I find, I want not to rush away from my reading. I like to linger when I can. The gentle joy and quiet awareness of the God who makes himself known makes it worth it.

Try this: Take your Bible passage from yesterday and let it guide your praying today. Then close your eyes, get comfortable, and simply, unhurriedly wait on the Lord. Let him remind you that those who turn to God "will be in awe and will tremble at the abundant prosperity and peace I provide" (Jer. 33:9).

## LESSON OF THE DAY

*Approach Bible reading as a conversation with God.*

## Pray the Promises

*God reveals wonderful possibilities through the words and prayers of the Bible.*

Does it seem that you are always improvising during your quiet times—and sometimes not particularly well? Do you long for confidence and conviction you cannot seem to muster on your own?

Spontaneity is wonderful in prayer. Knowing that you can say anything and everything to God gives you glorious freedom. But sometimes you need, like a budding writer, more than a blank page staring you down, waiting to be filled. You don't want to feel that your prayers are invariably impromptu talks. You need instruction, a coach, an outline. You need reminders to include the things your limited view might overlook. You may even need help with the words themselves.

I remember when my daughter, Bekah, now six, was first learning to talk. For all her earnestness, her words came out mostly as mumbling inflection and haphazard sound.

She needed many "big people" talking around her for her jabbering to grow into real language. So when she was not quite a year old, I would often say "Daddy" when I held her. I wanted her to imitate the sound. Sometimes I would say, "I love my Da-Da!" hoping she would repeat it after me. And she did! Not perfectly. Not with full comprehension. But one day I could make out her "I la la da da!" I was thrilled. And when she would see me after I had been away for a time, she would say, "Da da." She began to talk by mimicking, by allowing her words to fall into pattern with mine and her mother's.

This is also how we learn to pray. "Repeating God's words after him," wrote German pastor Dietrich Bonhoeffer, "we begin to pray to him,"[1] just as Bekah did her best to repeat my words after me. This means that when you pray during your quiet time, you don't always have to "start from scratch." You need not feel a constant burden to summon eloquence or generate momentum. It is not just up to you to get prayer started. When our feelings fail, when our words need a lodestar, when we lose assurance about what we say, we pay attention to the guidelines God has given. This he has graciously, wonderfully done in the Bible. We turn to Scripture to find there not only teaching *about* prayer but wonderful patterning and substance for our own stammering efforts. We find what Peter Kreeft has called "the prayers God wrote for us."[2]

This aid to my quiet times comes in two ways:

## PRAY THE SCRIPTURES

One of the most transforming insights for my prayer times came when I realized that I could not only read the Bible, but I could *pray* it. Personalizing and turning the psalms, hymns, stories, and teachings of the Bible into prayers will guide and strengthen your praying. You will experience the wonderful assurance that you are praying as God intends. In a sense you've already done this in the "spiritual reading" of the last two days. But praying the Scriptures is so valuable, so full of promise for anyone's praying, that it deserves a more detailed treatment. Sometimes you may be reading along or listening to a Bible passage being read aloud, and you find yourself wanting to claim its truth as your own. Today's exploration will help you do so.

Some of the most obvious candidates for praying the Scriptures are the passages where we see prayer actually taking place. I have more than once, for example, taken the apostle Paul's' words in Ephesians 1:17–19 as the basis for prayer: "I keep asking," Paul prayed, "that the God of our Lord Jesus Christ, the glorious Father, may give you the Spirit of wisdom and revelation, so that you may know him better. I pray also that the eyes of your heart may be enlightened in order that you may know the hope to which he has called you, the riches of his glorious inheritance in the saints, and his incomparably great power for us who believe." Instead of merely reading this as Paul's prayer, I change the pronouns: "I keep asking that you, the God of our Lord Jesus Christ, the glorious Father, may give Tom the Spirit of wisdom and revelation. . . ."

Or take these verses from a psalm that my wife and I prayed over one another not long ago when we needed spiritual refreshment:

> Guard my life, for I am devoted to you.
>> You are my God; save your servant [insert name]
>>> who trusts in you.
> Have mercy on me, O Lord,
>> for I call to you all day long.
> Bring joy to your servant [name],
>> for to you, O Lord,
>> I lift up my soul (Ps. 86:2–4).

You need not limit yourself to just the prayers of the Bible. Wonderful scriptural statements can also form a basis for meaningful prayer. "My soul finds rest in God alone; my salvation comes from him," as Psalm 62:1 affirms, can be more than a theological statement. Turn it into a prayer: "Lord, I need to find my rest in you." You might even go beyond that spare variation to say more: "Thank you, Lord, that you provide rest for my agitated soul. You save me and hold me close. I praise you."

---

Try this: Find a prayer in the Bible and pray it. Consider the verses from Ephesians 1 mentioned above. Or any number of the Psalms. Other prayers may be found in Exodus 15:21 (Miriam's song of praise), 1 Kings 8:21–30 (Solomon's prayer on behalf of the people), Psalms 51:1 (David's prayer for forgiveness), Mark 9:24 (a prayer for deeper faith), Colossians 1:9–13 (Paul's description of his prayer for the people's wisdom), or Romans 12:33–36 (where Paul glorifies God).

## PLEAD THE PROMISES

Closely related to praying the Scriptures, but with a different flavor, is what some call praying God's promises. The idea is to take an assurance from God and *stand* on it in prayer. "Tarry at a promise," Dwight L. Moody said, "and God will meet you there." With this way of praying you are beginning with what you know God has already said he will do. Your *application* of the promise may not always be on target, but the general direction of your prayers, focused as they are on God's self-revelation in the Bible, will be.

Prayer writer Armin Guesswein told how he discovered the power of such praying; the transformation, he said, came when he heard an elderly man praying at a prayer meeting:

> When he prayed, I detected something new. . . . It was not only fervency—I had plenty of that. Heaven and earth got

together at once when he prayed. There was a strange immediacy about it....

Eager to learn his secret, I went to see him one day. His name was Ambrose Whaley, and everyone called him "Uncle Am." He was a retired blacksmith—also a Methodist lay preacher. I soon came to the point: "Uncle Am, I would love to pray with you." At once he arose, led me outside across the driveway into a red barn, up a ladder, *into a hay-mow!* There, in some old hay, lay two big Bibles—one open. *What is this?* I thought. I prayed first, as I recall it. Poured out my heart, needs, burdens, wishes, aspirations, ambitions to God. Then he prayed—and there was "that difference" again. There, in that hay, on our knees, at the eyeball level, I said: "Uncle Am, what is it?... You have some kind of a secret in praying. Would you mind sharing it with me?"

I was twenty-four; he was seventy-three (he lived to be ninety-three), and with an eagle-look in his eyes, he said: "Young man, learn to plead the promises of God!"

My praying has never been the same since....

Uncle Am would plead Scripture after Scripture, reminding [God] of promise after promise, pleading these as a lawyer does his case.... He taught me the secret of intercessory praying.[3]

This suggests wonderful possibilities for your praying, for the Bible has promises applicable to every circumstance and need. Concerned about finances? Spend some time praying Matthew 6:33: "But seek first his kingdom and his righteousness, and all these things will be given to you as well." Jeremiah 29:11 provides a promise when you are needing guidance: "For I know the plans I have for you," declares the LORD, 'plans to prosper you and not to harm you, plans to give you hope and a future.' Or turn to Philippians 4:6–7: "Do not be anxious about anything, but in everything, by prayer and petition, with thanksgiving, present your requests to God. And the peace of God, which transcends all understanding, will guard your hearts and your minds in Christ Jesus." When you need healing, read and pray through James 5. When you are suffering, claim the promises of Romans 8 or 1 Peter.

And be open to how God may unexpectedly meet you through his promises. The other day I had a few minutes in the office of a staff member of my church, waiting for a meeting. I decided to use the time to pray for the promotion and distribution of a just-published book I wrote. Was word about the book getting out? Would it be noticed and reviewed? I was anxious. But then my eyes fell upon a verse on a poster tacked on the office wall: "The battle is not yours, but God's. . . . You will not have to fight this battle" (2 Chron. 20:15, 17). I believe God gave *me* a promise through those verses intended for the people of Israel millennia ago. I told God that I trusted him to fight the battle for me. I still worry sometimes, still wonder how the book will do. But I have a promise to claim as I pray. Whatever comes, I know that God is active.

Take heart! Just as the goodness of God is inexhaustible, so also are the Bible's promises, ones that make for fruitful, faithful praying.

Try this: Spend some time today reflecting on, and praying through, a promise of Scripture. If you need help getting started, choose a passage from those suggested above. Tell God, "I receive this promise. I believe that you can do what you pledge to do." Use the very words of the Bible to fill out your prayer.

## LESSON OF THE DAY

*God reveals wonderful possibilities through the words and prayers of the Bible.*

# Make Friends with Silence

*Quiet can make what we say and pray all the more profound.*

A friend of mine recently experienced a small miracle in her quiet time. Perhaps you will identify with her.

"I was off in my bedroom, by myself, folding laundry," she recalled, "watching a local news program full of blood and guts. I've been trying to pray more, and I suddenly realized I had a wonderful opportunity presenting itself." Louise turned off the TV, opened the window, and let in the warming breezes of a Chicago spring afternoon. She noticed the birds singing outside. A stillness settled on her. She prayed. "It was just five fleeting minutes—my four-year-old son discovered me and came barging in—but within those silent moments I felt a wonderful sense of God's presence."

Based on the last several days of material, you might conclude that your part in praying is mostly about what you say or do. But if you stopped there, how much you would miss! A rich devotional life also has much to do with what you *don't* say. In prayer, we often experience much by not doing; we often express more when our words are few. Sometimes the most profound moments in your relating to God happen when you get out of the way.

Today I want to encourage you to include breaks of restful, waiting silence. It is no accident that we speak of *quiet* times. One of the simplest and most important things you can do before God is simply to be still.

Just this morning I began my prayer time a bit agitated. I found myself pulled internally in different directions, my mind still in gear from getting my daughter out the door to school, my thinking filled with the calls I had to make, the editorial deadlines I'm facing. I had trouble focusing. Part of me wanted to be doing anything *but* praying. But I found the presence of mind (and soul) to close my eyes, get comfortable in my chair, and ask for God's help in stilling the mental flurry. When my mind wandered, I gently said, "Lord." I tried not to fill the time with verbal calisthenics. I rested. I became, on a human level, empty of words and fine phrases.

But that made the difference. Far from finding that a lack of talky exuberance dampened my prayers, the Lord began to fill the spaces left open for him. The quiet that settled over my soul helped me to calmly move on and read the Bible, pray for my friends and family, and spend time with my journal. I became aware that God was close.

Many spiritual teachers through the centuries have made similar discoveries. Biblical writers often use words like *silence* or *silent* to suggest an attitude of profound seeking. They use the words to call God's people from their preoccupations to better attend to God. "Pay attention, Job, and listen to me," said the Lord, "be silent, and I will speak" (Job 33:31). Lamentations says, "It is good for a man to bear the yoke while he is young. Let him sit alone in silence, for the LORD has laid it on him"

(3:27–28). And Habakkuk told the people, "the LORD is in his holy temple; let all the earth be silent before him" (2:20).

Jesus himself often withdrew to a "solitary place," away from the clangorous demands of others (Mark 1:35). On another occasion, because so many people were hounding them, Jesus said to his disciples, "Come with me by yourselves to a *quiet* place and get some rest" (Mark 6:31, emphasis added). In the center of active ministry and faithful service we find Jesus protecting moments for silence. He modeled a refusal to let life be consumed by a clattering, constant stream of demands. With my restless heart and chattery mind, I need what Jesus patterned.

Talk of silence sometimes leaves Christians with mixed feelings, however. It seems to resemble the meditative practices of Eastern religions. And it is true that some have advocated cultivating silence as a prelude for a trance-like state that counterfeits authentic spirituality. But what I mean is no esoteric practice for restless mystics. The point of silence is not unnaturally "blanking the mind," but quieting our hearts. Stopping our incessant mental activity lets us cultivate readiness. Silence is a classical discipline of the Christian life. After all, the psalm tells us to "be still" so that we come to "know God." Silence simply prepares our noisy, restless hearts for the gentle presence of God, a God who feels no need to shout over the sound barriers we erect.

We see this in some of the great figures of spiritual life. "Saints listen for the sights and sounds of God," writes Calvin Seminary professor Cornelius Plantinga. "They quiet themselves into a kind of absorbency, a readiness to hear the word of God, and also the voice of God, and even some of the silences of God."[1] Holy people don't blast their way into a room. They operate from a restful, secure lack of showy aggrandizement.

Silence also helps us to not be so scattered. Often we need to hush the clamor of voices that would derail our devotion. We need to push aside the bustling activities, the demands of others, the incessant drive to accomplish. Only then can we find a depth that goes deeper than surface words. One monk in the early centuries of Christianity put it: "When the door of the steambath is continually left open, the heat inside rapidly escapes through it; likewise the soul, in its desire to say many things, dissipates its remembrance of God through the door of speech, even though everything it says may be good.... Timely silence, then, is precious, for it is nothing less than the mother of the wisest thoughts."[2]

But how do you *practice* silence? Most of us are not accustomed to becoming still in this way. Our wordy, information-infatuated culture conspires against our faltering efforts. We are out of practice. But remember these pointers as you think about quietness of soul today:

## 1. LET GO

One trouble we have with silence has to do with our tendency always to "take charge." Just as we rely on words to manage and control others, we prefer to come into God's presence with gabby self-possession. Silence, however, places us before God with no words to hide behind. We leave behind our efforts to justify ourselves or inform God of our "terms." Silence requires trust. It asks us to not worry about not getting everything laid out and said just so. No wonder Jesus so often told his disciples, "Do not worry." No wonder the Bible stresses God's great love. We find courage to sit quietly, expectantly, in God's presence when we believe we are loved and welcomed. We no longer feel compelled to bluster our way through prayer. We lay down our guard.

## 2. REST IN GOD

With good news for any whose life is a scramble of activity, Jesus said, "Come to me, all you who are weary and burdened, and I will give you rest" (Matt. 11:28). Prayer need not resemble our furiously busy lives. God knows that just as our bodies need adequate sleep, so our spirits need replenishing pauses. We can relax. At least some of your quiet time should flow out of a holy ease. There should be an unruffled calm.

Paradoxically, this is all the more true (and all the harder) when my life seems flooded with appointments and urgent tasks. While the trajectory of my life would leave out quietness, I determine nevertheless that I cannot do without its refreshment. So I take refuge in a God of rest. I resist letting the day's tasks squeeze out time to sit lovingly in God's renewing presence.

## 3. COME BACK TO A QUIET CENTER

It is one thing to guard pools of quietness while at prayer, but what happens when we walk back into the scenes of daily life? Can we maintain our spiritual wits? Will our inner selves become as noisy as our surroundings?

It is possible, I believe, to carry a quieted heart into the fray and not lose perspective. "In quietness and trust is your strength," Isaiah 30:15 tells us. That holds not just for the mountaintop excursion but also for the daily walk. Thomas Kelly found this. He offers good advice on how to let quietness before the Lord pervade our lives:

How, then, shall we lay hold of that Life and Power? . . . By quiet, persistent practice in turning all of our being, day and night, in prayer and inward worship and surrender, toward Him who calls in the deeps of our souls. . . . An inner, secret turning to God can be made fairly steady, after weeks and months and years of practice and lapses and failures and returns. . . . Begin now, as you read these words, as you sit in your chair, to offer your whole selves, utterly and in joyful abandon, in quiet glad surrender to

Him. . . . Admit no discouragement, but ever return quietly to Him and wait in His Presence."[3]

–––––––––––

Try this: In today's devotional time, begin by simply sitting quietly. If thoughts stream at you, if words rush in to fill the spaces, return your focus to God by gently repeating a simple name for God: Lord, Jesus, Father. Set apart ten minutes for quiet communion with God, unworried by words and unhurried by any agenda. Then carry on with your normal praying.

## LESSON OF THE DAY

*Quiet can make what we say and*
*pray all the more profound.*

# Listen to God's Still, Small Voice

*God has some things to tell you;*
*take time to listen.*

The other morning my prayer time began in an unusual way. Before I was barely awake, I sensed the Lord catching my attention. I felt he wanted to tell me something. There was no audible voice, just a sense that I should listen, even as I lay in bed. I expected a dramatic word, but what happened was quite simple, really: I felt impressed to pray for a friend of mine with a grave case of lupus. As I prayed I detected a gentle nudge to find a piece of stationery and jot her a note of encouragement. As the day went on, through meetings and errands and conversations, I tried to listen. I felt guided in small matters. My waking exercise in listening was modest and uncomplicated. I may never fully know how God used my heeding attitude. But I believe it was important.

If you are like me, your approach to God may habitually stop just short of listening. You may become so aware of what you want to ask that you neglect to wait to hear how God answers. Yesterday's experiment in making friends with silence will go a long way in setting the stage for listening. Ah, but how to *do* it? How can we begin listening, right where we are—ordinary people living everyday lives?

Here are two pointers:

## RECLAIM THE IMPORTANCE OF LISTENING

You may need reminding—even convincing—that listening belongs in your quiet times. You may have mixed feelings about the whole idea.

Who of us, for example, has not known or heard of someone who strutted around saying, "God said we should do it *this* way." The person's certitude over a supposed word from on high made him or her impervious to discussion. Or we see someone justify silly behavior with a "God told me so." We don't want to repeat their errors. If we try to listen, we reason, what if we don't get it right?

Or you may have heard some Christians conclude that God has said all that needed saying—two thousand years ago. He stopped talking much when Jesus ascended and the Bible was compiled. Our listening, they argue, will be confined to what we read in revealed Scripture. Or perhaps God communicates through ethical principles or through a pastor or religious leader. But a specific, personal word? That would smack of mysticism or wishful thinking.

Then again, part of you may worry, What if I pause to listen, and *actually hear?* "My concern is not that God won't show up," a friend once confessed, "as much as that he *will*. That scares me." The God of the universe, after all, beggars our comprehension. He is not one to take lightly or play games with. We know we are not worthy. So will he meet us in kindness? We need a settled conviction that God will plan good for us. That what he might say will ultimately help and heal. That even if we need a hard word, God's love will make it possible to do what he summons.

The best answer to such hesitations, I believe, comes from the realm of relationship. If, as Christians believe, God is more than a mute deity or vague force, why *wouldn't* he speak? The God of the universe is also the Shepherd of my little world. And if he wants to speak, it will be in ways consistent with what we know about a God who so loved the world that "he gave his one and only Son, that whoever believes in him shall not perish" (John 3:16). In other words, as involved as God is in the lives of his children, he has no reason to leave us without special guidance.

So we listen by first recalling that a God of love waits to communicate. We remember that prayer need not—should not—be a monologue. God will not be stingy in communicating his purposes. He will get through. Willow Creek pastor Bill Hybels once recalled, "As I've studied prayer and prayed, I've sensed God saying, 'If we enjoy a relationship, why are you doing all the talking? Let *me* get a word in somewhere!'"[1]

Such is the picture we get in Scripture. God spoke directly, personally, specifically to people throughout its pages. The word *listen* appears 332 times in the Bible, *more times* than the word *speak*. The word *hear* appears even more frequently. Clearly, we are creatures built for listening, not just talking. And if God tells us to listen, surely he will not leave us hanging. "For Zion's sake I will not keep silent," he said through the prophet. "For Jerusalem's sake I will not remain quiet" (Isa. 62:1). And the prayer of young Samuel, "Speak, for your servant is listening" (1 Sam. 3:10) is one God ever delights in answering. While we may need to tune in, while he rarely shouts, God gladly approaches us with what Elijah discovered was a "gentle whisper" (what the King James Version translates as a "still small voice") (1 Kings 19:12). No wonder my friend Steve Brown likes to say that he often does his best praying when he *stops* praying. That's when God can finally respond.

## CULTIVATE AN ATTITUDE OF LISTENING

In learning to listen, there is a place for fasting (doing without food for a set time) or other rigorous disciplines of the spiritual life. But the most important thing, for now, is to come with an unguarded, humbled heart. Simply express to God your desire to hear. You are not demanding or manufacturing something. You are giving permission. You are leaving room for an articulate God.

My friend Diane Eble recently wrote of receiving an advertisement in the mail for a device that, when plugged into an electrical outlet, would turn the electrical system of a house into a giant television antenna, boosting reception. "I don't know if it works," she wrote. "But it reminds me of the fact that the signals are out there, in the air." What determines the outcome is what happens on the receiving end.[2]

Of course, you are already listening every time you prayerfully read the Bible. You have opened yourself to however God might speak through his revealed Word. But ask God for help in specifics. Pray for help in tuning in through the circumstances of your life, for instance. God may already be hitting you over the head through events and doors that open or close. The ordinary can be an instrument for conveying the extraordinary. The books you stumble across, the things your children say, the turns your career takes—through all of these and more God may whisper his unfolding will.

And then invite God to speak directly to your heart and will. Quiet your racing thoughts and listen for that deeper Voice. Seek God's help in sorting through the many feelings and impulses so you can discern which are truly of him. Ask him to speak about specific areas. Depending on your situation, consider questions like these:

- What is the next step in my job? Am I doing your will here?
- Where should I be going in this dating relationship (or marriage, or relationship with another family member)?
- Am I spending enough time with my children (or others who depend on my care)?
- How much should I be giving to the church and charities?
- Are there ways in which my attitude needs improvement?
- Am I being too hard on myself and not trusting in your forgiveness?

Then wait in trust. Don't be concerned if you hear silence. God is not a jukebox into which we put change and wait for a mechanical response. He is a living being, a *sovereign* God. He will answer in good time, sometimes letting us know only what we *need* to know, not always what we think we'd *like* to know.

Keep in mind, too, that we need coaches to help us when our own wants and whims interfere with our reception. We need the steadying feedback of others who can help us weigh and learn to recognize the Voice of the Good Shepherd. We will not always hear clearly or even accurately, especially at first, but we can grow and develop in our sensitivity.

Finally, remember that guidance is part of a larger picture. Our listening for God's voice grows out of a certain kind of life, one that philosopher Dallas Willard describes as "a life of loving fellowship with the King and his other subjects within the Kingdom of his Heavens." God's answers are not something we seek only when anxious. We are not about extracting a word from God as much as submitting lovingly to his grand purposes. God's guidance is intended to develop, says Willard, "into an intelligent, freely cooperative relationship between mature persons who love each other with the richness of genuine ... love." We are not about twisting God's arm but seeking his desires. "Only so," says Willard, "will guidance itself come out right."[3]

---

Try this: After spending time talking to God and reading Scripture, tell God you are ready to listen. Let him know that you want his will to be done. Invite him to convey anything you need to know to live faithfully during the day. You may even try asking for his insight on some specific area. Don't be discouraged if you seem to hear nothing. God may communicate in unseen, unnoticed ways. He may wait until you are even more ready for the answer. The important thing is to ask and seek, and know that you will not be left directionless.

## LESSON OF THE DAY

*God has some things to tell you;*
*take time to listen.*

# Devote a Quiet Time to the Lord's Prayer

*The Lord's Prayer offers lessons from the Master Prayer himself, Jesus.*

Bekah, my six-year-old, is learning to read. She has a tiny book that contains a simple children's version of the Lord's Prayer. Something she did with it the other night reminded me of a truth about prayer.

She came for bedtime prayers with the book in hand. She wanted to read it out loud for her part in our nightly family custom. Now, you should know that her reading vocabulary is small. She couldn't even make out the first word. But she bravely began. My wife, Jill, sitting beside her, prompted her: "Dear Father ..." Bekah got the next two words, "in heaven," as well as the next page's line. But the phrase after that was a struggle. On it went. Jill supplied fully half of the words as Bekah read. Jill coached her. Coaxed her. Helped her get her prayer out.

I realize how like Bekah we are. For all your grown-up polish, you may still sometimes find yourself intimidated by the prospect of praying. The desire is there, but the facility is not. You sit down to pray and feel a mass of feelings and scattered thoughts. You may not know where to begin. How do you bring sense and order to it all?

Jesus' earliest followers shared in your struggle. "One day Jesus was praying in a certain place," Luke tells us. "When he finished, one of his disciples said to him, 'Lord, teach us to pray, just as John [the Baptist] taught his disciples'" (Luke 11:1). They wanted guidance, too! In a prayer outline recorded in slightly different forms in Luke and Matthew, Jesus gave his followers a wonderful framework for praying. It is a revelation to many to discover that this prayer can be more than a ritual, more than a hastily recited rote prayer. The Lord's Prayer can wonderfully orient and organize your quiet time today. It contains astonishing riches. The great themes of prayer and devotion are here: praise, confession, petition, thanksgiving. It has a sequence and arrangement brilliant in its simplicity. Jesus, the Master Prayer, makes the basics of prayer wonderfully accessible.

Of the two versions of the prayer recorded in the Gospels, Matthew's is the best-known and most often quoted. From Matthew 6:9–12, here is a sampling of its life-changing themes, followed by practical advice on how to *pray* it.

### Our Father in heaven

How we address God carries great significance. This is not the first time in the Bible that God is named Father, but before this, God's people used the term in a national or corporate sense—God as the Father of *Israel,* or as the Father of a chosen king like David. But with Jesus the meaning becomes wonderfully personal. *Individuals* like you and me, and churches like yours and mine, can freely name God as Father. On the strength of Jesus' teaching and modeling, New Testament writers even referred to God as *Abba,* an affectionate term akin to our *Daddy* (see Romans 8:15, Galatians 4:6). We need not exhaust ourselves to get the attention of this loving, fatherly God. From the first sound on your praying lips you affirm that God will greet you with kindly, parental care.

## Hallowed be your name

This loving God—even his name—is to be revered. To speak of a *name* meant a great deal to the ancients. It was not merely the tag by which to call a person, it conveyed the character of the individual. It communicated something of the person's essence. So the psalmist could pray, "Those who know your *name* will trust in you" (Ps. 9:10, emphasis added). And here in Jesus' prayer we are reminded that God's name—his reputation—will be vindicated. It will be acknowledged as holy (see also Ezekiel 36:22–28). To *hallow* is to treat differently, to give a unique and special place to something. We are asking that God be given the preeminence he deserves—by us and by others.

## Your kingdom come

Jesus here reminds us that God is establishing his rule, and that we have a role in praying for its advance. This kingdom is both here (in part) and at hand (in its fulfillment); both now and coming. So while we know that, in Jesus, God's kingdom has arrived, we also await Christ's return for its completion. While we do, we pray that God speed its coming. We not only ask for "kingdom come" in some grand sweeping sense but also for our own spheres of work and relationships. And we are praying, whether we realize it or not, for our own submission to God's purposes.

## Your will be done on earth as it is in heaven.

"There can now be no grander prayer," fourth-century monk John Cassian said, "than to wish that earthly things be made equal with heavenly things."[1] Here we ask God to make a part of our daily lives what is already celestial reality. Praying in this way acknowledges that obedience to God's will, not our whims, matters most. We voice our hope that our desires and actions line up with God's.

## Give us today our daily bread.

This is a simple request for God to make sure that we have the things we need for the coming day. There are long traditions of interpretation that suggest this bread is that of the Lord's Supper, or Jesus himself, the *bread of life* (John 6:33–35). But the simplest and most obvious explanation is that Jesus here sanctifies our asking for everyday things, for the shoes and pans and walls we need to live and work and be. We are not here asking for bulging bank accounts or more than we need but for that which sustains our physical existence.

## Forgive us our debts, as we also have forgiven our debtors.

Jesus helps us confront our failure to "pay" that which is due—to God, others, ourselves. We fall short, we fail to become all God wants, for all our prayers that God's will be done. Jesus helps us face the inevitable reality that we are not perfect.

And he reminds us through this prayer that unforgiveness on our part toward others puts us in a condition in which we cannot accept forgiveness from God. In contrast, to receive divine forgiveness is to put us in a frame of mind to offer human forgiveness. They intertwine.

## And lead us not into temptation, but deliver us from the evil one.

The idea is to ask that God help us not succumb to temptations or trials. It is not saying that God tempts us (James 1:13 tells us explicitly that he does not). The sense of this statement is that God has power to rescue us. He can even deliver us from the designs of the "evil one" (the Devil). Paul put it like this in his letter to the Corinthians: "And God is faithful; he will not let you be tempted beyond what you can bear. But when you are tempted, he will also provide a way out so that you can stand up under it" (1 Cor. 10:13). Here we ask for God's empowering and his protection that we may stand firm when the going gets difficult or our moral resolve weakens.

**For yours is the kingdom and the power and the glory forever. Amen.**

You will not find this phrase, so common in the traditional spoken (and sung) version of the Lord's Prayer, in many modern Bible translations. It often appears only in a footnote. Why? There is some question as to whether it really was in the original prayer Jesus gave his followers. But the thought behind it certainly fits and sums up the whole prayer. We here affirm that all begins and ends in the Creator, Sustainer, and Completer of the universe. This is a paean of praise and adoration, an ascription of blessing to one who exists in inexpressible goodness and might. We are "giving" to God what is already his, declaring his ownership and stewardship of everything. It ends our prayer on an appropriate note of triumph.

## MAKING THE LORD'S PRAYER YOUR OWN

All these praises and petitions, I find, can give my longings focus, helping me to think through the issues and urgencies of the day. They keep my prayers from littleness or stagnant sameness.

So try to really *pray* this prayer! Someone once asked a nineteenth-century spiritual teacher about cultivating a deeper prayer life. She is said to have replied, "Say the Lord's Prayer, but take an hour to say it."

Take the phrase *Our Father in heaven,* for example. I sometimes use it as a springboard: "It's good to know you are in heaven, Lord," I might say, "that whatever else that means, you are above the push and pull of my little world. That you are aware of all that happens around me." Or I make the plea for God's forgiveness a prod to admit before God my own sins, my own debt to his grace.

I find such a guide helpful when I am unable to sleep. Or when I find my mind wandering. Our praying of it need not be a slavish occupation. We need not pray the whole prayer each time. It sometimes happens that I get so caught up in one of the petitions that I forgo the others. Many are the times I have gotten no further than the first phrase or two, so caught up was I in prayerfully pondering God's fatherhood.

---

Try this: Review the phrases of the Lord's Prayer above (or from memory) and spend a few moments with each one, allowing it to nudge your praying in the directions Jesus suggests. Make sure that you move from the general ideas into specifics in your own life. Allow what may have been for you a recited prayer to become a deeply personal, day-to-day practical guide for richer praying—praying Jesus-style.

## LESSON OF THE DAY

*The Lord's Prayer offers lessons from the Master Prayer himself, Jesus.*

# Experiment with a Journal

*"Take notes" on what God is doing in your life.*

Do you ever absentmindedly neglect to pray about some of the important things going on in your life? Perhaps you forget to offer thanks for yesterday's blessings. Or you simply wish you grasped better what God was up to through life's turns and detours. You want help in keeping it straight. For years I have used a simple practice that helps me in precisely these ways: I keep a journal. Because of the truth of the Chinese proverb that the finest mind is less reliable than the simplest ink, the act of writing (and later reading) may help you also.

I am not talking about an elaborate practice suitable only for those who think they have a way with words. No, what I am about to describe may require little more than keeping an up-to-date prayer list. Or you may want to write paragraphs of prayers, insights from Scripture, and reflections on events. You may use a bound book created just for the purpose or keep a few slips of paper in your Bible. You may write every day or much less frequently. But just as talking and listening are important activities for a devotional life, so also may writing and reading become tools to keep you on track. Jotting down prayers, tracing their answers, and taking notes on what you hear and see God do in your life may well enrich your times with God.

## WRITING CAN HELP YOU PAY ATTENTION TO LIFE'S DAILY EVENTS.

You may not realize how significant some incidents are—at the time. But whether today holds a miracle or a mere whisper, a milestone or only a faint sign of movement, what happens to you *matters*. God communicates not only through his Word, not only through a still, small voice, but through the people you meet, a letter from an old friend, the job a company offers you, the frank word your spouse shares, or the pangs of conscience that beset you. On a seemingly uneventful day, who knows what grand purposes are set in motion? Writes novelist and pastor Frederick Buechner, "Before the sun sets every evening, [God] speaks to each of us in an intensely personal and unmistakable way. His message is not written out in starlight, . . . rather it is written out for each of us in the humdrum . . . events of each day."[1]

How often have I been moved to read back in journal entries from years ago my earliest successes and setbacks as a fledgling writer. How was I to know the importance of those first letters accepting (and rejecting) my magazine articles? As the years went on, as the journal pages accumulated, I chronicled my struggles and longings when a calling to pastoral ministry steadily transfigured into a call to a writing ministry. A book on prayer I read here, a seminar on the spiritual life I attended there, a sense of leading I felt more than once soon confirmed my calling to call people to prayer through the written word.

## WRITING CAN HELP YOU BECOME MORE HONEST WITH GOD

The Psalms abound with gritty honesty. Our own writing helps us, as King David wrote, "search" our hearts (Ps. 4:4; see also Psalm 139:23) and know what is within us.

Gordon MacDonald discovered this: "When I felt empty or defeated, I talked about that too in the journal. Slowly I began to realize that the journal was helping me come to grips with an enormous part of my inner person that I had never been fully honest about. No longer could fears and struggles remain inside without definition. They were surfaced and confronted."[2] Letting our struggles find words can often put us in touch with our deepest feelings—and God's truest purposes for us in the midst of them. Our honest grappling on paper with doubt, guilt, anger, and impure desires can even yield new insights. Sometimes we are helped to see ourselves as we are.

## WRITING CAN HELP YOU REMEMBER GOD'S FAITHFULNESS

Remembering is more important than we sometimes think. The Bible summons us to "watch yourselves closely so that you do not forget the things your eyes have seen or let them slip from your heart" (Deut. 4:9). Psalm 77:11 declares, "I will remember the deeds of the LORD." Indeed, some of the Psalms can be read as a kind of journal that called the people to remembrance. They record wondrous ways God moved to answer his people's prayers. Journaling can be a way of remembering God's actions in our lives, taking to heart his guidance, recording answers to prayers, and ensuring that we do not forget what he is about. Keeping a journal is a disciplined form of remembering.

A move my family and I made some years ago provides a case in point. We moved to a Midwestern community out of a sense of call to join a church there. Little was settled in terms of jobs and finances. But we had a clear sense that we *should*. During our preparations for moving, I would often read through previous years' journal entries to remind myself how God had been faithful before. It helped me more surely believe that God could be trusted for the present.

Often I have turned to another entry from a February day. Driving to a hospital to visit a church member in for surgery, I wrote of an experience of prayer, of "a flowing sense of joy, . . . an inward exuberance" as the Holy Spirit lifted my prayer beyond words. It was something of a breakthrough that enriches my praying to this day. The encounter lives more vividly in my mind and soul for having been recorded, read, and reread.

---

Try this: Take a sheet of paper and date it at the top. Try writing down at least one insight, request, or answered prayer. You may want to write out the names of the people you regularly pray for. Or simply write about the significant relationships, encounters, and settings of today. Don't just record events but include your feelings—and especially your spiritual perspectives. Don't worry about being eloquent. And don't feel self-conscious out of a mistaken sense that anyone else needs to read this. Be honest. Be prayerful. At the end of several days, reread your entries. Do you detect any patterns? Does God seem to be telling you something? Try experimenting with your journal each day for the coming week.

## LESSON OF THE DAY

*"Take notes" on what God is
doing in your life.*

# Let Others' Prayers Jump-Start Yours

*When you can't find the words, try someone else's.*

By now you have discovered that inspiration doesn't always appear on demand. On occasion you may even have felt spiritually tired. Or you sensed that your view of things needed a wider horizon. In that case, as you have seen, praying the Lord's Prayer and other biblical prayers can bring renewing power and refreshing perspective. But there is yet another resource. Printed or "book" prayers can become a scaffold, a supporting framework, to strengthen you. They help you tap into the wisdom of another faithful soul. They can inject new meaning into your times with God.

Surprised? Most of us prefer spontaneous praying. "Programmed" prayers, we fear, lock us in and squeeze out room for the Holy Spirit. Speaking to God in the words of another may seem like secondhand devotion. Or like turning to a textbook to find the right formula when off-the-cuff, heartfelt words would be more appropriate. But model prayers help you articulate the yearnings of your heart when words don't come easily. They can "prime the pump" when you don't feel like praying.

And there is another benefit: Many of the church's great prayers span centuries and form a cross section of divergent places. Using them helps you draw from a wealth of experience and insight. Some were penned by those whose faith was tested by fire, others by wise, gentle pastoral shepherds. Some come from times of war, others from spiritual awakenings. Some from faraway lands, others from compatriots. Visionaries, poets, and working people all have left a legacy. Availing yourself of such a deep reservoir of devotion is not second-class praying!

So how can you use them?

*First, see these as a supplement to your own words*—your own praises and confessions and thanksgivings and petitions. We are not talking about a vicarious spirituality that must always have the form and configuration just so. Use these as a natural addition to your regular prayer practices.

*Second, try including a single prayer every now and then* when you have your quiet times. Below I include a few actual prayers. Experiment!

*Third, read slowly, meditatively.* Better to prayerfully read one short prayer than hurriedly run through a dozen. The goal is to make the prayer your own.

*Fourth, concentrate on the meaning.* Older prayers may strike you (or distract you) by their archaic vocabulary. But don't spend too much time on the quaintness of expression or, on the other hand, the beauty of the words. Glean the meaning.

*Finally, ask God to make your use of such prayers meaningful.* Don't assume that what you take away from such prayer hinges only on you or your concentration. God can infuse the form, bringing life to mere words, through his Holy Spirit.

## SAMPLE PRAYERS

Here are some prayers you might consider using for today. In some cases I have noted the author and the century to suggest the breadth of representation. Skim them all (or a few) and settle on one or two to make your own. Feel free to come back to these pages in coming days.

**A prayer to use as you begin to pray:**

Almighty and everlasting God, you are always more ready to hear than we are to pray, and to give more than we either desire or deserve: Pour upon us the abundance of your mercy, forgiving us those things of which our conscience is afraid, and giving us those good things for which we are not worthy to ask, except through the merits and mediation of Jesus Christ our Savior; who lives and reigns with you and the Holy Spirit, one God, for ever and ever. Amen.[1]

**A prayer to help you dedicate yourself fully to God:**

Almighty and eternal God, so draw our hearts to you, so guide our minds, so fill our imaginations, so control our wills, that we may be wholly yours, utterly dedicated to you; and then use us, we pray, as you will, and always to your glory and the welfare of your people, through our Lord and Savior Jesus Christ. Amen.[2]

**A prayer of praise to God (Francis of Assisi, thirteenth century):**

You are holy, Lord, the only God. You do wonders.
You are strong, you are great, you are the most high,
You are the almighty King.
You, Holy Father, are the King of heaven and earth.
You are Three and One, Lord God of gods.
You are good, all good, the highest good,

Lord God, living and true.

You are love, charity.

You are wisdom; you are humility; you are patience;

you are beauty; you are meekness; you are security;

you are inner peace; you are joy; you are all our riches.

You are enough for us. . . .

You are the protector,

you are our guardian and defender;

you are strength; you are refreshment.

You are our hope, you are our faith, you are our charity,

you are all our sweetness,

you are our eternal life:

great and wonderful Lord,

God almighty, merciful Savior.[3]

**A prayer to see God's glory (A. W. Tozer, twentieth century):**

Heavenly Father: Let me see your glory, if it must be from the shelter of the cleft rock and from beneath the protection of your covering hand, whatever the cost to me in loss of friends or goods or length of days let me know you as you are, that I may adore you as I should. Through Jesus Christ our Lord. Amen.[4]

**A simple prayer to say throughout the day (Eastern Orthodox, sixth and seventh centuries):**

Lord Jesus Christ, Son of God, have mercy on me.

**A prayer of reminder (John Donne, sixteenth and seventeenth centuries):**

O Lord, never allow us to think that we can stand by ourselves and not need you.

**A prayer when you need guidance (Basil, fourth century):**

O Lord, our God, teach us, we beg of you, to ask you in the right way for the right blessings. Steer the vessel of our life toward yourself, tranquil haven of storm-tossed souls. Show us the course in which we should go. Renew a willing spirit within us. Let your Spirit curb our wayward senses and guide and enable us unto that which is our true good, to keep your instructions, and in all our works evermore to rejoice in your glorious and gladdening presence. For yours is the glory and praise from all your saints, for ever and ever.

A **prayer for true devotion** (**Susanna Wesley, nineteenth century**):

Help me, Lord, to remember that religion is not to be confined to the church or closet, nor exercised only in prayer and meditation, but is everywhere I am in your presence. So may my every word and action have a moral content.[5]

A **prayer of commitment** (**Thérèse of Lisieux, nineteenth century**):

My God, I choose the whole lot. No point in becoming a saint by halves. I'm not afraid of suffering for your sake; the only thing I'm afraid of is clinging to my own will. Take it, I want the whole lot, everything whatsoever that is your will for me.[6]

## FOR FURTHER READING (AND PRAYING)

Collections of prayers should be available at your Christian bookstore or the religious section of a well-stocked general bookstore. Hymnals and worship books also usually contain prayers useful for Christian devotion. Perhaps the best-known is the Episcopal *Book of Common Prayer.* Many of the older devotional writings, such as Augustine's *Confessions,* also contain moving prayers. Another source is printed devotional aids such as *Our Daily Bread, The Upper Room,* and *My Utmost for His Highest.* These and other daily devotionals (which usually contain teaching, Scripture readings, and printed prayers) can be incorporated into regular quiet times.

———————

Try this: Take at least one of the prayers above and say it slowly, reflectively. Take time with each phrase, filling it out with your own personal concerns as you feel led.

## LESSON OF THE DAY

*When you can't find the words,*
*try someone else's.*

# Find a Friend

*Spiritual growth is not a do-it-yourself project.*

Some years ago I took up furniture making. My first projects were simple: wall candleholders cut from pine, bookends made from dowels and old barn siding. I did pretty well on my own. When I ran into problems, I consulted woodworking books or copied others' projects; it was a mostly solitary hobby. But then I got more ambitious: I tackled building a loveseat for our living room. The construction, I quickly discovered, required complex joints and precise finishing techniques.

That's when I turned to Marshall, a member of my church who is experienced in crafting fine furniture. Marshall not only advised me about screws and miter cuts, he invited me over to his home workshop to use his power planer, a piece of equipment I could never buy for my modest shop. He even guided my hands as I made my first cuts. Without his coming alongside, I would never have created a lasting piece of furniture.

I suspect you have already discovered the need for people who play a similar role in your spiritual growth. You look for someone who can answer your questions, show you how it's really done, even encourage you when you bog down. You want guidance and support.

Your experience is more common than you may think. "A soul that remains alone," wrote the sixteenth-century monk John of the Cross, "is like a burning coal that is left by itself: It will grow colder rather than hotter." We need the spiritual warmth that comes from other hearts that burn for God. We need fellow believers who walk with us as companions on the way. Using varied imagery, Ecclesiastes 4:9–12 tells us,

> Two are better than one, . . .
> his friend can help him up.
> But pity the man who falls
> and has no one to help him up!
> Also, if two lie down together, they will keep warm.
> But how can one keep warm alone?
> Though one may be overpowered,
> two can defend themselves.
> A cord of three strands is not quickly broken.

But we have hesitations in turning to others for help. Although we say we don't like the sound of going it alone, we don't always nurture friendship and fellowship. We have many close acquaintances but few confidants. Rarely does a coffee hour or fellowship meal at church allow us to tell another much more than the headlines of our lives. We shake hands but rarely speak deeply. Where do you go when you have struggles? A frontier ideal of rugged individualism whispers in the ear that it is "weakness" to seek another's help, that if I have a problem, I should try harder—on my own.

There is a better way. All through the Bible we see and hear encouragement to turn to others. The fabled partnership of

Ruth and Naomi, the friendship of David and Jonathan, or the mentoring of Paul and Timothy point to our need to not walk solo. It is no accident that Jesus sent out his seventy-two followers in *twos* (Luke 10:1). "Follow my example," Paul told the Corinthians, "as I follow the example of Christ" (1 Cor. 11:1). "Where two or three come together in my name, there am I with them" (Matt. 18:20). Sometimes the Bible is even blunt: "Let us not give up meeting together, as some are in the habit of doing, but let us encourage one another—and all the more as you see the Day approaching" (Heb. 10:25). And through the millennia that have followed, spiritual teachers have urged the faithful to learn from others. "He becomes the disciple of a fool," Bernard of Clairvaux tersely said centuries ago, "who sets up to be his own teacher."

Even when you have your quiet times with God alone, don't think that you are not a part of a community. Every solitary prayer has a communal backdrop. The influence, training, modeling, and support of others live on in us in sometimes hidden but always significant ways. So allow your hunger for another's hand or counsel to lead you to the encouragement and accountability you need.

Here's how:

## TURN CHURCH-GOING INTO A SPIRITUAL EXPEDITION

You may go to church for many reasons, but this Sunday make growing in spiritual depth a key motivation. As you sing, pray with others, listen to Scripture, ponder a sermon, and share your spiritual gifts, ask yourself, *What can I learn about praying more faithfully?* Stay open to something someone may say—from a pulpit or off the cuff—that can help you seek God when it's time to pray on your own. Jot down at least one insight on a notecard or sheet of paper. Tuck it in your Bible until your next quiet time with God. Contemplate what you wrote and pray about how God might take you even deeper.

## TURN CASUAL CONVERSATION INTO HOLY LISTENING

So often our day-to-day talking skims the surface; we hear about things that happen, but only rarely about the things that matter deeply. This week try to gently turn a corner in at least one encounter. Steer the conversation to spiritual concerns. Keep your ears and eyes open to what you can learn. Or tell a Christian friend that you are praying for him or her and that you believe prayer matters. You may hear an update on how to pray more specifically. Or find someone whose faith you admire and "interview" that person. Ask, "What have you learned about prayer?" or "How have you struggled with quiet times with God?" You might even mention what you wrestle with yourself and ask for the person's insight—and prayers. Doing so may not be easy, so promise yourself you will take the risk of going deep.

## TURN EVERYDAY FRIENDSHIP INTO LIFE-CHANGING FELLOWSHIP

Every day we rub shoulders with committed Christians from whom we can learn—the neighbor with whom we have coffee, the partner at the office, the roommate who shares our apartment, the member of our Bible study group. Many of these could teach us something about prayer. Some could even become mentors or prayer partners. They need not be theology professors, just have a heart devoted to Christ and a desire to grow in grace. Nor do they need to be pastors or missionaries to have experiences to relate, convictions to share, and encouragement to give.

Small groups can offer the same opportunities to learn from others. House-church meetings, Bible studies, Cursillo or Emmaus renewal weekends, and small prayer breakfast groups afford times of sharing, feedback, and prayer for individual needs. They can encourage you and even hold you more accountable.

"Always take counsel with a wise and conscientious [person]," said Thomas à Kempis, "and desire to be instructed and governed by others rather than to follow your own ingenuity."[1]

Inviting someone to help us grow in prayer is no panacea, of course. Tensions may arise in any friendship or fellowship. But the companionship we seek, and sometimes give to others, holds the promise of making our quiet times richer and more satisfying.

---

Try this: Consider times recently when you said to yourself (or another), "I wish I had someone to talk to about my spiritual struggles." Take time in your quiet times to think about (and perhaps jot down) some of your greatest needs for growth. Now think about how the fellowship of Christ and the friendship of a brother or sister can help you in your need. Be willing to take risks in seeking the accountability and support only another can impart.

## LESSON OF THE DAY

*Spiritual growth is not a do-it-yourself project.*

# Draw Near to God Through Music

*Hymns and songs can enrich your quiet
times, turning them into personal worship.*

If you have any church experience at all, you
have sung praises to God in corporate worship. But you may not have mined music for
*personal* worship. If not, you are about to discover how *sung* prayer can enrich your times
with God.

I speak from personal experience. Recently
I've been battling discouragement about a set-
back on a major writing project. On a deep
level I have sensed that the proper response
was to praise God in faith and trust. But it was
not easy. The *feelings* behind my adoration of
God hung back; I said my praises, but dutifully.
Then I realized something that made all the
difference: I could *sing* my praises to God; the
melody and rhythm could carry my words
(and my reluctant feelings) along. I began to
find myself lifted out of my self-imposed discouragement.

There's something about singing, when the
melody matches the words and catches the

sentiment, that helps us pray and worship. Music adds another dimension, a parallel expression. Just as the artful playing of a symphony sometimes effortlessly takes wing, so using music in your praying may help your spirit to soar. And it can allow truths to penetrate to a depth not always touched by words alone. Music can help your quiet times when you do two things.

## LEARN ABOUT THE CENTURIES-DEEP MUSICAL ROOTS OF GOD'S PEOPLE

Employing music in praise and prayer is no new discovery. You can easily trace it to early biblical times. You find music at many of the celebrations or milestones of life: A farewell might include "joy and singing to the music of tambourines and harps" (Gen. 31:27) and a welcome might include the sound of tambourines (Judg. 11:34). Daily work might be accompanied by the songs or chants of well diggers (Num. 21:17–18) or of those treading grapes (Jer. 48:33). Battles, particularly victories, provided numerous occasions for song. As the Israelites walked from Egyptian slavery to freedom, Miriam sang,

> Sing to the LORD,
>     for he is highly exalted.
> The horse and its rider
>     he has hurled into the sea (Ex. 15:21).

And at worship, of course, the people sang regularly and vigorously. The words *sing* or *song* appear more than one hundred times in the Psalms alone. As you read the Psalms, you can almost hear the faint traces of tambourine and plucked strings. We are told in Psalm 100:1–2,

> Shout for joy to the LORD, all the earth.
> Worship the LORD with gladness;
>     come before him with joyful songs.

Psalm 81:2 commands,

Begin the music, strike the tambourine,
play the melodious harp and lyre.

And in Acts 16:25 we see a jailed Paul and Silas, praying and singing hymns to God at midnight, and "the other prisoners were listening to them." In their need and longing, even after Paul and Silas had been "severely flogged," they could not keep from singing.

The biblical writers knew that music has power to communicate at a level more profound than words, more lofty than speech. "He who sings prays twice," I once saw on a poster. Through centuries of musical expression in the church, music has become a kind of prayer itself, expressing our deepest longings. Whether through medieval Gregorian chants or a revivalist's altar-call hymn singing, music leads us to drop many of the defenses that would keep worship a merely intellectual exercise. No wonder hymn writer Isaac Watts once said, "The singing of God's praise is the part of worship most closely related to heaven." We find ourselves caught up to a new wonder. Our communion with God is carried along. And our quiet times can benefit.

———

Try this: Take one of the above biblical passages related to employing music in praise and worship and look it up in your Bible. Read some of the surrounding verses. Get a feel for the larger setting for the words. Then take a moment to reflect on how God seems to *like* for us to approach him with songs and music.

## EXPERIMENT WITH SINGING AND MUSIC TODAY

It's one thing to realize the biblical and Christian precedent for music. But even more important is its practice. Hymns, praise choruses, even free-form singing can lend new freshness to your times with God. Try it! Get a hymnbook or book of worship choruses and *sing* your prayers and praises. Or if you play an instrument, make a musical offering to God, expressing your soul's joys and longings. Or find a tape or CD of praise music and play a song or two as you begin your quiet time.

Consider these examples from real life:

- This morning, while I did my stretching exercises and calisthenics, I decided to play a CD of praise and worship music. The phrases of the songs, "Soften my heart, Lord," or "There's no one like you, my Lord," lent a more reverent feel to my running and my praying.
- One morning a man I know found himself singing the hymn "Dear Lord and Father of Mankind." He had not even thought of the hymn for months, but the third stanza, describing Jesus in prayer to the Father, "resonated," he said, "with something profound inside." His day was not the same for his having rediscovered an old hymn that he turned toward God as prayer.
- I have another friend, a musician, who sometimes sits at his piano when the house is empty and "plays" his prayer. He begins with a simple worship song and uses that as a launching point for a more free-form, spontaneous time, playing his piano and singing his prayers. "Sometimes," he says, "I make up my own words. Sometimes I just play and don't sing at all. But I know God hears it as a prayer."

As in so many areas, the point is not technical proficiency but a heart eager to express what God is due. The other day my experimenting took me into the simplest kind of singing you could imagine: I took the phrase "I love you, Lord," and simply sang it in a free-floating melody I "composed" as I sang. It would win no music awards, but it *felt satisfying*. I offered my voice up to God and approached him, as the Bible encourages us to do, with song. It need not be more complicated than that!

Or perhaps you would like to see your aspirations stretched. Turn to some of the great hymns of the faith: "O Master, Let Me Walk with Thee," " Be Thou My Vision," "How Great Thou Art." If you play an instrument, consider using it as a vehicle to express your longing, contrition, or praise.

And during the day, let a hymn or song run through your mind. Just as a popular song from the radio can repeat itself in your mind, even without your bidding, let the songs of faith fill your consciousness throughout the day.

Try this: Take a favorite hymn or worship song, close your eyes, and let your singing be your prayer. If you play an instrument, you may want to play it. Whatever you do, do it to the glory of God. Let your time with music this morning set the stage for the rest of your prayer time.

## LESSON OF THE DAY

*Hymns and songs can enrich your quiet times, turning them into personal worship.*

# Invite a Child into Your Devotional Time

*Delight in the simplicity of a child's prayer.*

Have you ever observed the exuberant abandon of a child?

Not long ago my wife and children and I made our way to the front rail of our church for Communion. Bekah, our youngest, broke off from us and *skipped* to the front, her arms flapping and flying at her sides, an impish grin on her face. At first I was taken aback (and embarrassed). After all, shouldn't the rite that memorializes our Lord's death proceed with a certain dignity?

But the more I thought about it, the more I could appreciate a child eagerly participating in worship. I had something to learn from Bekah's infectious abandon. It was all the more true, given that this was the Sunday after Easter and we were still celebrating Jesus' resurrection.

Children have a surprising amount to teach about matters of the Spirit. They model growth in intimacy with God. And they may be able to help you in your own devotional times. It can be no accident that the words *child* or *children* appear almost a hundred times in the four Gospels. Jesus had a special place in his heart for children and a keen sense that they can teach us about worship and prayer. Consider these passages:

- Jesus said, "I praise you, Father, Lord of heaven and earth, because you have hidden these things from the wise and learned, and revealed them to little children" (Matt. 11:25).
- [Jesus] called a little child and had him stand among them. And he said: "I tell you the truth, unless you change and become like little children, you will never enter the kingdom of heaven. Therefore, whoever humbles himself like this child is the greatest in the kingdom of heaven" (Matt. 18:2–4).
- People were bringing little children to Jesus to have him touch them, but the disciples rebuked them. When Jesus saw this, he was indignant. He said to them, "Let the little children come to me, and do not hinder them, for the kingdom of God belongs to such as these. I tell you the truth, anyone who will not receive the kingdom of God like a little child will never enter it." And he took the children in his arms, put his hands on them and blessed them (Mark 10:13–16).
- But when the chief priests and the teachers of the law saw the wonderful things [Jesus] did and the children shouting in the temple area, "Hosanna to the Son of David," they were indignant. "Do you hear what these children are saying?" they asked him. "Yes," replied Jesus, "have you never read,

  'From the lips of children and infants
      you have ordained praise'?" (Matt. 21:15–16).

Are you surprised at the prominence of children in Jesus' ministry? There's more. One of the New Testament's favorite images for our standing before God is that of *children*. "The Spirit himself," writes Paul in Romans, "testifies with our spirit that we are God's children" (Rom. 8:16). And John's Gospel talks about our becoming "children of God" (John 1:12). Such language reveals a conviction that children exemplify the way we should live before our heavenly Father.

But how can children help you to *pray*?

I think of three characteristics:

## SIMPLICITY

At their best, children remind us that prayer can be unaffected, unadorned, even blunt. Most children haven't learned to decorate their prayers with verbal ornamentation. They tend to get to the point and say what's on their heart. And they realize they are not self-sufficient; they do not labor under the delusion that they are the captains of their souls, which gives them an unaffected expressiveness to God. Take this prayer from a little boy named James Kennedy:

Dear God,

I am sorry for being naughty today.

Please make me a better boy tomorrow.

Bless all my family and friends. Amen.[1]

His prayer models the kind of humble simplicity that surely was part of what Jesus had in mind when he said we must receive the kingdom of God like a child to enter it. You may see the exuberance of children as an interruption to your worship or prayer times. But Jesus said, "Let the little children come." He knew their prayers have a freshness and directness that adults should emulate.

## WONDER

We live in times, a friend of mine likes to say, more characterized by "Blah" than "Ah!" We need our capacity for astonishment renewed. And children, with their perceptiveness, their insatiable curiosity, their unhurried fascination with the world, can help point the way. It does us good to watch children and follow their lead in exploring and responding to the joys of living. Children don't always fit nicely into our regimented schedules, but sometimes their delighted awe in a just-fallen autumn leaf or a strain of symphonic music teaches us to allow ourselves to take time. For my daughter, the advent of fireflies this summer has become an event. I might enjoy their lights at times; I can appreciate the way they sparkle unexpectedly in the dusky warmth. But Bekah loves to run in the yard where they appear, trying to catch and cup in her hands the glowing bugs so she can see their simple glories up close. She might not right then utter a prayer of thanks to their Creator, but surely her reverent joy is a kind of thank-you.

"Some years ago, when our children were young," writes one mother,

> we moved to the Southwest. The children were very excited and spent the first days in their new home, exploring and marveling at all the wonderful things they were seeing for the first time. One late afternoon, our son Tim, who was three years old at the time, was playing in the yard. Suddenly the door burst open, and he rushed in exclaiming, "Come quick and see, Mom. The sunset is all over the place." Indeed, those southwestern sunsets are something to behold, and as I ran outside and viewed the sky, a sense of wonder and awe filled me. If Tim had not called my attention to it, I probably would not have noticed the sunset. I was too busy unpacking boxes.[2]

**TRUST**

We adults say we believe in prayer, that great things through it are wrought. But children often model it unself-consciously. They have not become too jaded to worry about the dilemmas of seemingly unanswered prayers.

My youngest son has health problems that sometimes make it hard for him to get to sleep at night. When he was younger, his fears of the dark unknowns of a still house sometimes drove him to our bedroom. Jill and I would suggest a number of coping techniques, such as turning on his bedside light and reading or watching a video in the family room. But Micah quickly came to discover the most effective tool of all: He would have us pray out loud for him. Almost always he would leave our room settled and able to face his restless fears. Soon he would be asleep. He knew we had asked, so he could let go. It was as simple as that. Even the daunting specter of fear and dark gloom would be made light.

Children, writes Betty Shannon Cloyd, "have a formula and it is simple: We have a need, we present it to God. God hears our prayers and God answers. In childlike faith, they present their needs to God trusting in a God who is able and willing to answer."[3] In so doing, they teach us a profound lesson about prayer.

I don't expect children to deliver reasoned discourses on the effects of petitionary prayer. There is a place for theology texts, for study. But we learn from children mostly by watching and doing as they do. It's simple and potentially life-changing.

Try this: If you have young children or grandchildren, try praying out loud with them. Encourage them to articulate their requests and prayers of thanks. Coach them if they feel a bit awkward praying out loud. And then listen.

If you are not around children in your day-to-day life, volunteer a Sunday at Sunday school or child care for toddlers and observe how children pray. Invite a child to say grace over a meal when a family with children visits.

Watch for at least one characteristic you can take into your own prayer times. And whether you are able to observe a child in prayer today or not, tell God that you long for the simplicity, wonder, and trust of a child. God, pleased to be our heavenly Father, will be sure to answer.

## LESSON OF THE DAY

*Delight in the simplicity of a child's prayer.*

# Dip into the Devotional Classics

*Learn from God's faithful witnesses through the past centuries.*

I entered my teen years in Southern California in the late 1960s. People were beginning to say that the old was definitely "out," that venerable teaching could not hold a candle to contemporary insight. The motto seemed to be, "Embrace the new, don't explore the tested and true."

Sound familiar, even today? Such thinking sometimes sneaks into the church. We forget that centuries of believers have struggled to pray and faithfully worship, that classical writings on the spiritual life convey a depth and power untouched by celebrity best-sellers. We live and work and pray surrounded by a great company of witnesses, but many modern Christians have never known the treasures of the lives and writings of those who have gone before. When they finally find their way to the classics, it is with great delight and discovery.

But a problem may confront you when you begin to dig in. The works of spiritual giants like Augustine, Brother Lawrence, Thomas à Kempis, Teresa of Ávila, Oswald Chambers, Amy Carmichael, and others may seem a bit intimidating at first. Sometimes the language seems dated, musty, the vision for the Christian life daunting, the thought forms a bit foreign. It doesn't take long to see that some effort will be called for. You may not feel ready to tackle an entire volume.

I understand that hesitation. It has taken a while for the classics of devotion to become a consistent, large part of my devotional life. Just the other day I picked up a work by the eighteenth-century French church leader Jean-Pierre de Caussade, *The Sacrament of the Present Moment* (also known as *Abandonment to Divine Providence*). I had picked it up a number of times over the years but never sustained enough interest to get beyond a few paragraphs. This time, though, my eyes fell on de Caussade's comments about Mary and Joseph, Jesus' parents. The family led an ordinary life, outwardly speaking, he said. "[Mary] lives quietly with Jesus and Joseph who work for their living." But there is something else. "What do they discern beneath the seemingly everyday events which occupy them? What is seen is similar to what happens to the rest of mankind. But what is unseen, that which faith discovers, is nothing less than God fulfilling his mighty purposes.... God reveals himself to the humble in small things—'He has filled the hungry with good things' (Luke 1:53)—but the proud, who only attach importance to outward appearances, cannot see him even in the big ones."[1] Immediately I realized how helpful de Caussade could be in my trying to become more aware of God's presence in the little things of life. In God's good timing, what I had previously passed over quickly suddenly became real. That can happen for you. Your life, and your quiet times with God, can be immeasurably enriched.

Consider these passages a sampling, appetizers to give you a simple entrée into some of the great works of devotion:

## AUGUSTINE, FOURTH CENTURY

"Great [are you], LORD, and mighty in power; [your] understanding has no limit" (Ps. 147:5). And people want to praise you, for they are a part of your creation; they carry their mortality with them and bear the evidence of their sin and the proof that you resist the proud. Still people want to praise you, we who are only a small part of your creation. You have prompted us, that we should delight to praise you, for you have made us for yourself and our hearts are restless until they rest in you.[2]

Late have I loved you, O Beauty so ancient and so new, late have I loved you. For you were within and I was outside myself, and I sought you there. Unlovely, I rushed recklessly among the lovely things you have made. You were with me, but I was not with you. These things kept me far from you; even though they did not exist unless they were in you. You called and cried aloud, and shattered my deafness. You flashed and shone, and chased away my blindness. You breathed fragrant odors and I drew in my breath, and now I pant for you. I tasted, and now I hunger and thirst. You touched me, and now I burn for your peace.[3]

## JULIAN OF NORWICH, THIRTEENTH CENTURY

Our soul is so preciously loved by the one who is highest that it is beyond the knowledge of all creatures. That is to say, there is no creature made that can understand how much and how freely and how tenderly our Maker loves us. For as the body is clothed in cloth and the flesh in skin and the bones in flesh and the heart in the torso, so are we, soul and body, clothed and enclosed in the goodness of God.[4]

## BROTHER LAWRENCE, SEVENTEENTH CENTURY

The holiest, most common, most necessary practice in the spiritual life is the presence of God, that is to take delight in and become accustomed to His divine company, speaking humbly and talking lovingly with him at all times, at every moment, without rule or system and especially in times of temptation, suffering, spiritual aridity, disgust, and even of unfaithfulness and sin.[5]

## OSWALD CHAMBERS, EARLY TWENTIETH CENTURY

God's training is for now, not presently. His purpose is for this minute, not something in the future. We have nothing to do with the afterwards of obedience; we get wrong when we think of the afterwards. . . . God's end is to enable me to see that He can walk in the chaos of my life just now. If we have a further end in view, we do not pay sufficient attention to the immediate present: if we realize that obedience is the end, then each moment as it comes is precious.[6]

We are apt to say that because a man has natural ability, therefore he will make a good Christian. It is not a question of our equipment but of our poverty, not of what we bring with us but of what God puts into us; not a question of natural virtues or strength of character, knowledge, and experience—all that is of no avail in this matter. The only thing that avails us is that we are taken up into the big compelling of God and made his comrades (see also 1 Cor. 1:26–30).[7]

## WHERE TO FIND THE CLASSICS

Most Christian bookstores have sections with books on prayer and devotion. You should be able to find a number of the classics. And the religion section of general bookstores usually has a number of classics written from a Christian perspective (mixed in with a grab bag of other religious perspectives, so exercise discernment). Abridgments and volumes that gather many excerpts from great devotional writers can also be found in many stores.

Any list of writers to start with will be hopelessly incomplete, but here are some you might consider:

Augustine, *Confessions*
Brother Lawrence, *The Practice of the Presence of God*
Julian of Norwich, *Revelations of Divine Love* (or *Showings*)
Thomas à Kempis, *The Imitation of Christ*
Dietrich Bonhoeffer, *The Cost of Discipleship*
Oswald Chambers, *My Utmost for His Highest*
Jean-Pierre de Caussade, *The Sacrament of the Present Moment*
A. W. Tozer, *The Knowledge of the Holy*
Amy Carmichael, *If, Candles in the Dark*
E. M. Bounds, *Power Through Prayer*
O. Hallesby, *Prayer*

Here are some compilations, some arranged with daily readings, that may provide an even better start for you:

*Life Renewal Devotional*, ed. Wightman Weese (Tyndale House)
*The Treasury of Christian Spiritual Classics* (Thomas Nelson)
*A Guide to Prayer for Ministers and Other Servants*, Rueben Job and Norman Shawchuck (Upper Room Books)
*Disciplines for the Inner Life*, Bob Benson, Sr., and Michael W. Benson (Thomas Nelson)

"Rekindling the Inner Fire" series, ed. David Hazard (Bethany House)

*Devotional Classics,* ed. Richard Foster and Jim Smith (HarperSanFrancisco)

## HOW TO READ THE CLASSICS

As with devotional Bible reading, reading the great writings of devotion goes better when you keep certain things in mind:

- *Read prayerfully.* The goal is not to impress anyone with your speed or intellectual comprehension but to hear God and experience his presence. This means bathing your reading in prayerful openness. Consider beginning with the sentiments of this prayer from the celebrated eighteenth-century writer Samuel Johnson: "Almighty God, our heavenly Father, without whose help labor is useless, without whose light search is in vain, invigorate my studies and direct my inquiries, that I may, by due diligence and right discernment, establish myself and others in your holy faith. Take not, O Lord, your Holy Spirit from me; let not evil thoughts have dominion in my mind. Let me not linger in ignorance but enlighten and support me, for the sake of Jesus Christ our Lord."[8]

- *Read in humility.* Remember while you read that our age has no monopoly on truth, that while the forms and language may seem antiquated, you may still be able to draw great insight. Whatever the oddities (or quaintness) of the writer's times, what they have to say may be a great gift.

- *Read with openness.* Ask yourself how what you are reading may be true of your own life. Let your mind be quickened. What new directions does the writer suggest? What would practicing the truth you find look like in your daily life?

Try this: Reread the selections above (or find your own passage from a favorite classic) and choose a section to ponder. Read it prayerfully, humbly, and openly, seeing what difference it might make in your daily life. Let what you read form the basis for the rest of today's prayer time.

## LESSON OF THE DAY

*Learn from God's faithful witnesses
through the past centuries.*

# Pray Your Way Through the Psalms (Part 1)

*The Psalms give us cue cards for honest personal worship.*

I'm not sure I should even be saying these things," a friend once confided about his prayers. There was a rawness to his vocabulary, a baring of his soul, blemishes and anger and all. He felt uncertain: "Is it okay to pray this way?"

Do you likewise wonder whether honest, blunt words really belong in prayer?

You should know that there is in the Bible one book distinguished from all the others by the fact that it contains almost nothing but prayers. And we are not talking about garden-variety, pious pleasantries. These are honest, even gritty prayers. They are perfect prayers when you are ready to get real with God in heartache, anger, or doubt. And they can form and shape your prayers into an authenticity many only dream of.

This has been the testimony of countless Christians through the ages. "Whoever has begun to pray [the Psalms]," wrote German pastor Dietrich Bonhoeffer, "will soon give a vacation to other little devotional prayers and say [with Martin Luther], 'Ah, there is not the juice, the strength, the passion, the fire which I find in the Psalter. It tastes too cold and too hard.'"[1] Pastor and professor of spiritual theology Eugene Peterson agrees. The Psalms keep us from "a series of more or less sincere verbal poses that we think might please our Lord."[2] We find, to our relief, the reassuring recognition that our emotions—extravagant, exhausting, exhilarating—need not be checked in at the door of the sanctuary or prayer-closet. Who we are and how we feel, in all our range of drives and complexities, belong in our praying.

Today's and tomorrow's chapters focus on the expanse of these emotions. Today we focus particularly on the troubling emotions, the ones we would like no one to know, that make us embarrassed or uncomfortable, the ones the Psalms tell us belong in our prayers, not just in our secret thoughts.

Here is a sampling of the Psalms to use for your quiet time today, each followed by a suggestion for prayer.

### Pain and Complaint

How long, O LORD? Will you forget me forever?
How long will you hide your face from me?
How long must I wrestle with my thoughts
and every day have sorrow in my heart?
How long will my enemy triumph over me?
Look on me and answer, O LORD my God.
Give light to my eyes, or I will sleep in death;
my enemy will say, "I have overcome him,"
and my foes will rejoice when I fall.
But I trust in your unfailing love;
my heart rejoices in your salvation.
I will sing to the LORD,
for he has been good to me.
(Ps. 13)

Try this: Think about a time, past or present, when difficulties made you wonder if God could be trusted. If you wonder now, let this prayer of David articulate your urgent need and hurt. Don't feel a need to rush too quickly to the triumphant, trust-filled conclusion. Spend some time letting this prayer open your heart to God.

### Absence and Longing

As the deer pants for streams of water,
    so my soul pants for you, O God.
My soul thirsts for God, for the living God.
    When can I go and meet with God?
My tears have been my food
    day and night,
while men say to me all day long,
    "Where is your God?"
These things I remember
    as I pour out my soul:
how I used to go with the multitude,
    leading the procession to the house of God,
with shouts of joy and thanksgiving
    among the festive throng.
Why are you downcast, O my soul?
    Why so disturbed within me?
Put your hope in God,
    for I will yet praise him,
    my Savior and my God. . . .
My bones suffer mortal agony
    as my foes taunt me,
saying to me all day long,
    "Where is your God?"

Why are you downcast, O my soul?
    Why so disturbed within me?
Put your hope in God,
    for I will yet praise him,
    my Savior and my God.
(Ps. 42:1–5, 10–11)

---

Try this: This psalm acknowledges those times when God seems distant or absent. We do not always live with a white-hot sense of God's nearness. The inner assurance of his presence may weaken. And yet the psalmist does not let that stop him from addressing God. He lets his longing drive him to God, not avoid him. Prayerfully read this psalm again, noting the rhythm of question and affirmation, longing and thanksgiving. Let it guide your own praying.

### Anger and Pleas for Vindication

Sing praises to the LORD, enthroned in Zion;
    proclaim among the nations what he has done.
For he who avenges blood remembers;
    he does not ignore the cry of the afflicted.
O LORD, see how my enemies persecute me!
    Have mercy and lift me up from the gates of death,
that I may declare your praises
    in the gates of the Daughter of Zion
    and there rejoice in your salvation. . . .
The LORD is known by his justice;
    the wicked are ensnared by the work of their hands.
But the needy will not always be forgotten,
    nor the hope of the afflicted ever perish.
Arise, O LORD, let not man triumph;

let the nations be judged in your presence.
Strike them with terror, O LORD;
    let the nations know they are but men.
(Ps. 9:11–14, 16, 18–20)

---

Try this: The faithful life is more than a pleasant stroll; sometimes others will oppose us. Enemies may intimidate us. Or we
may see the wicked prosper. These stiff verses, sometimes troubling to Christians for their severity, remind us that we can be
passionate about God's honor. We need not be passive in our
lives or in our praying when the unjust try to harm God's faithful or circumvent God's purposes. As you prayerfully reread this
psalm, ponder how God might be giving you permission to care
deeply and vigorously for the triumph of justice and good.

## LESSON OF THE DAY

*The Psalms give us cue cards*
*for honest personal worship.*

# Pray Your Way Through the Psalms (Part 2)

*The Psalms help us bring a wide range of emotions to our devotions.*

Emotions—even, as we saw yesterday, our harsh ones—belong in our prayers. But the sentiments that drive us to prayer are not, by themselves, an adequate *basis* for prayer. For all the seeming urgency of our emotions, taking our emotional temperature will not always properly guide our praying. Our feelings need a larger context.

Some days I sit down with the Psalms and find myself praying something I never would have thought of, something that was precisely what I needed to contemplate.

We may need to utter prayers of confession, for example, precisely when we feel most self-assured. We may need to praise God the most when we feel discouraged and want to do nothing but complain. Or when the future is rosy, we may need to remember the cost of faithfulness. Sometimes we need our words stretched, our feelings nudged in new directions. The Psalms help us offer devotion that is not pieced together like a crazy quilt of emotional fragments. Praying our way through them helps keep us out of spiritual ruts.

As you pray the Psalms, you discover that no situation in your experience goes without some parallel prayer in the Psalms. "It is my view," wrote Athanasius, fourth-century bishop of Alexandria, "that in the words of this book the whole human life, its basic spiritual conduct and as well its occasional movements and thoughts is comprehended and contained. Nothing to be found in human life is omitted."[1] No wonder the Psalms are said or sung every Sunday in some churches. In the ancient church it was not unusual for people to memorize the whole of the Psalms! In one of the Eastern Orthodox churches candidates had to memorize the Psalms before becoming pastors. The Psalms were seen as a school of prayer.

We can pray without them, of course, but with them we find our prayers given form, substance, breadth. We need not pray the Psalms all the time, but with them we connect our daily emotions to some larger scheme. Certainly we should pray our way through them every now and then.

Note these movements and how they can expand your praying today:

### Joy and Praise

My heart is steadfast, O God;
   I will sing and make music with all my soul.
Awake, harp and lyre!
   I will awaken the dawn.
I will praise you, O LORD, among the nations;
   I will sing of you among the peoples.
For great is your love, higher than the heavens;
   your faithfulness reaches to the skies.
Be exalted, O God, above the heavens,
   and let your glory be over all the earth.
(Ps. 108:1–5)

Try this: Reread these verses, then close your eyes and spend a few moments praising God in your own words.

### Guilt and Confession

Have mercy on me, O God,
   according to your unfailing love;
according to your great compassion
   blot out my transgressions.
Wash away all my iniquity
   and cleanse me from my sin.
For I know my transgressions,
   and my sin is always before me.
Against you, you only, have I sinned
   and done what is evil in your sight,
so that you are proved right when you speak
   and justified when you judge.
Surely I was sinful at birth,
   sinful from the time my mother conceived me.
Surely you desire truth in the inner parts;
   you teach me wisdom in the inmost place.
Cleanse me with hyssop, and I will be clean;
   wash me, and I will be whiter than snow.
Let me hear joy and gladness;
   let the bones you have crushed rejoice.
Hide your face from my sins
   and blot out all my iniquity.
Create in me a pure heart, O God,
   and renew a steadfast spirit within me.
Do not cast me from your presence
   or take your Holy Spirit from me.
Restore to me the joy of your salvation
   and grant me a willing spirit, to sustain me.
(Ps. 51:1–12)

Try this: Let this psalm be the occasion for you to prayerfully ask God if there are any areas in your life that need to be confessed, forsaken, and forgiven.

### Anxiety and Trust

O LORD, the God who saves me,
 day and night I cry out before you....
From my youth I have been afflicted and close to death;
 I have suffered your terrors and am in despair.
Your wrath has swept over me;
 your terrors have destroyed me.
All day long they surround me like a flood;
 they have completely engulfed me.
You have taken my companions and loved ones from me;
 the darkness is my closest friend.
(Ps. 88:1, 15–18)

Try this: Let this psalm give you permission to share with God situations that leave you anxious or frightened. Be sure to return to the first verse for its reminder that God is indeed one who hears and saves. Move from your time of praying these psalms to intercession for the people for whom you regularly pray.

## LESSON OF THE DAY

*The Psalms help us bring a wide range of emotions to our devotions.*

# Come to God with a Newspaper in Hand

*Take the sorrows and needs of the world to God and turn them into fervent prayers.*

You don't have to read many headlines or watch many news broadcasts to conclude that the world aches for redemption. Bombings, scandals in high places, spiritually lost entertainers, starving children, and warring nations remind us how, in Paul's words, "the whole creation has been groaning as in the pains of childbirth right up to the present time" (Rom. 8:22).

Perhaps you find it discouraging, even depressing. You would just as soon forget the bad news—all the more when you come to your devotional times. Shouldn't praying give us sanctuary from the stress and upheaval? Besides, what difference will the quiet of one person's prayers make against the juggernaut of violence and godlessness?

Or perhaps the news leaves you with a different struggle. You see stories of children orphaned by an accident, or a cancer patient battling for life, or a company victimizing and exploiting workers. You want not just to sit and sympathize. Something in you longs to help, to *do* something. *If only I could make a difference!* you say to yourself. But you don't know how or even where to begin.

Whatever your hesitation or concern, prayer for the world's heartaches or the crises next door lets you participate in furthering God's kingdom. "More things are wrought by prayer than this world dreams of," wrote Alfred, Lord Tennyson. Our devotions have far-ranging impact. They affect the outcome of distant events and daily happenings. We pray for souls, by all means, but also for God's will to be done on *earth*, in desperate situations. We pray for the needy, the hungry, the disconsolate. We pray for peace. We ask for God to reconcile what has been put asunder. We make praying an opportunity for *connecting* with a world in need, not simply retreating from it.

It may surprise you to discover the relevance your devotional times have to the very things you hear on the news. Someone once said we should come to our devotions with a Bible and a newspaper. He believed we need both to serve God faithfully. He meant that we need to pray globally and locally. Believing in God does not mean turning our backs on the world but opening our hands and hearts toward it in compassionate prayer. The tragedies, crises, and temptations around us provide grist for prayer for all believers, not just social activists. So wrote Paul to young Timothy, "I urge, then, first of all, that requests, prayers, intercession and thanksgiving be made for everyone—for kings and all those in authority, that we may live peaceful and quiet lives in all godliness and holiness. This is good, and pleases God our Savior" (1 Tim. 2:1–3).

We follow, after all, one who said that he came "to preach good news to the poor ... to proclaim freedom for the prisoners and recovery of sight for the blind, to release the oppressed"

(Luke 4:18). Through Isaiah the prophet, God spoke of a fast (going without food) that went far beyond mere spiritual sentiment but drove us into involvement in the world:

> "Is this the kind of fast I have chosen,
>> only a day for a man to humble himself?
> Is it only for bowing one's head like a reed
>> and for lying on sackcloth and ashes? . . .
> Is not this the kind of fasting I have chosen:
> to loose the chains of injustice
>> and untie the cords of the yoke,
> to set the oppressed free
>> and break every yoke?"
> (Isa. 58:5–6)

Draw close to God, in fact, and you will find yourself drawn out to compassion for others. The God who rises with healing in his wings comes also as a goad when I am indifferent about my neighbor. Communion with Christ will create compassion in us. We will *want* to pray for a world in need. The sixth-century monk Dorotheus of Gaza pictured the world as a large circle with God in the middle of it. Human beings, he said, start their lives at the circle's edge. As we grow closer to God, making our way to the circle's center, we also move closer to one another. One leads to the other.

With this in mind, try two things today:

*Come to prayer with a newspaper (or news magazine) in hand.* Leaf through it, letting the stories remind you of situations needing help and, most likely, desperately needing prayer. That story about a convicted murderer, for example, gives you an opportunity to pray for his or her redemption. When the story mentions family members of both criminal and victim, remember them. Or when you read about bloodshed in a far land, the pro-life efforts of a local group, a world leader's peacemaking trip, persecuted missionaries, or the problems of gang violence and drug trafficking, include those concerns. Be specific. Preface your prayers with an acknowledgment that God is powerfully at work in the world. Reread 1 Timothy 2:1–3, quoted in part above, and remember that your prayers are part of a long stream of the church's centuries of prayer for the world. Then pray! (Caution: It's easy to get drawn into a juicy story and get distracted from the purpose at hand!)

*Come to your newspaper or news broadcast with prayers in your heart.* This may well be a project for another part of the day. As you drive to work, for example, your regular radio station may carry a news break. Perhaps you are the kind of person who watches the evening news or relaxes with a newspaper. As you read or listen or watch, rather than just shake your head in exasperation, let your taking in become an act of prayer. Become an active participant, sanctifying time that might otherwise be an exercise in morbid curiosity. Consider jotting down items for continued prayer. And you may consider doing what a friend of mine has done for years: She "adopts" entertainers and other prominent people for special, ongoing prayer, asking God to bring them to salvation. Make prayer a lifestyle, something integrated into your interaction with the world around you.

Prayer, after all, confers on us incredible opportunity and awesome responsibility. Folding our hands in prayer is no act of resignation. It does not lead us to accept every circumstance with an overly spiritualized calm. Rather, it leads us into a world of need. And, because of God's power at work in our prayers, a world of possibility.

## LESSON OF THE DAY

*Take the sorrows and needs of the world to God and turn them into fervent prayers.*

# Experiment with Varied Approaches

*Avoid the slavery of habit and convention.*

If anything squelches a growing devotional life, it's the idea that there is only one way, one routine, one approach. The good news is that you don't have to be a slave to the way "it's always been done." The devotional life can partake of great variety.

Don't feel constant pressure to innovate. Perpetually experimenting and never establishing solid habits will only leave you tired. I can testify to the healthy place of a routine; I don't want always to have to figure out what, where, and when in my quiet times. Patterns create a certain freedom.

But allow yourself some room for variety. Especially when things seem stale, try some new approaches. Just as one coping method for burnout at the office is to rearrange your desk, just as taking a new route in your daily commute to work may help you arrive refreshed, bringing a new angle to devotions may help renew your devotional energy. Today we'll take a quick, guided tour of two ways of varying your times with God.

## TRY A NEW POSTURE

If our culture knows any posture for praying, it is lowering the head (preferably with eyes closed) and folding the hands. But in the Bible you encounter a wide range of postures and positions for praying. Here is a sample:

*Kneeling.* "Come, . . ." says the psalmist, "let us kneel before the LORD our Maker" (Ps. 95:6). You may think this a bit old-fashioned, but kneeling continues as a Sunday morning worship custom in a number of denominations, such as the Episcopal Church. Try kneeling during *your* quiet times. Something about the humility implied in this position reminds us that we come before God relying on his grace, honoring his majesty.

*Lifting hands.* In recent years charismatics have revived this ancient posture. It has clear precedent in the Old and New Testaments:

Hear my cry for mercy
    as I call to you for help,
as I lift up my hands
    toward your Most Holy Place.
(Ps. 28:2)

When I was in distress, I sought the Lord;
    at night I stretched out untiring hands.
(Ps. 77:2)

I want men everywhere to lift up holy hands in prayer, without anger or disputing.
(1 Tim. 2:8)

Lifting your hands before God exemplifies openness. It contrasts in a very physical way with clenched, tightly held hands. It points us to God, ready to receive what he has, symbolizing our trust and praise of a glorious God.

*Lying prostrate.* We Americans tend to be reserved and dignified in the ways we carry ourselves. But dignity is scant virtue in the presence of God. And there is something graphic, something profound about laying ourselves out on the floor before the Lord. In 1 Chronicles 29:20, David told the assembly gathered for worship, "Praise the LORD your God." Then, we read, "they all praised the LORD, the God of their fathers; they bowed low and fell prostrate before the LORD and the king." When we do likewise, we declare our utter dependence on God, our utter willingness to lay our very selves before him, with no vestige of haughtiness. We thereby honor God with our bodies, not just our words.

*Standing.* "Stand up and praise the LORD your God," the people were told in Nehemiah 9:5. And the psalmist speaks of his "feet standing on level ground" as he praises the Lord in the "great assembly." Standing signifies our readiness and alertness. Like kneeling, it is a sign of respect, one worthy of our offering God when we come to him in prayer and worship.

---

Try this: Decide on a posture mentioned above for your quiet time today. Use one or more of the forms of prayer discussed on earlier days, but this time do it while kneeling, uplifting hands, lying prostrate, or standing. You may even employ a combination: kneeling while you confess your sins and seek God's forgiveness, then standing while you praise God for Christ's mercy.

## TAKE A PRAYER WALK

You may assume that quiet times will always be stationary. But I often pray while I go running in the morning, and walking can similarly stimulate the body while the soul seeks God's face. In doing so we pray with eyes wide open; we not only lift up our daily concerns, we also find ourselves reminded of God's creative handiwork in the world around us. If you can walk or run in a place not crowded with traffic and blaring horns, all the better, but even a walk down a busy Manhattan street reminds us of God's creative hand.

The great church reformer John Calvin frequently referred to the world as a "theater of God's glory." The beauties of creation testify to God's goodness. After all, in the opening sentences of the Bible, says Eugene Peterson, "God speaks a world of energy and matter into being: light, moon, stars, earth, vegetation, animals, man, woman."[1] We are first introduced to God in the very tangible realm of matter and substance, rocks and rivers, not disembodied concepts. Creation therefore reminds us constantly of God. "Wherever you cast your eyes," wrote Calvin, "there is no spot in the universe wherein you cannot discern at least some sparks of his glory."[2]

A quiet time provides the perfect time to become reacquainted with the wonders of God's world. "Earth's crammed with heaven, . . . And every common bush afire with God," penned Elizabeth Barrett Browning. When we pray with our eyes open and our bodies surrounded by beauty, we will see that. We will be reminded of the power and greatness of the Creator. And we will not only enjoy the beauty of his presence, but we will be led to honor the hand behind the handiwork.

Try this: Read the following verses from Psalm 19:

The heavens declare the glory of God;
the skies proclaim the work of his hands.
Day after day they pour forth speech;
night after night they display knowledge.
There is no speech or language
where their voice is not heard.

Their voice goes out into all the earth,
   their words to the ends of the world.
(Ps. 19:1–4)

Complete your quiet time today with a brief walk or run outdoors. (Perhaps the best you can manage is a brief sit on your front porch or a few minutes by a window. Or perhaps you need to plan a time when you can experience the evidences of God's glory in creation for an extended time.) Whatever you do, take time to recall today that "the heavens declare the glory of God." And let what you see point you in praise and thanksgiving to God, the God who made it all, and who made you.

## LESSON OF THE DAY

*Avoid the slavery of habit and convention.*

# Lay Out a Realistic Plan

*Don't fail to plan.*

I once read a wonderfully thorough book on the spiritual life. It explored every conceivable kind of prayer. It inspired me to try different ways of praying. It left me in awe of the range possible. But it also left me frustrated.

Chalk up part of my difficulty to spiritual denseness. Perhaps now I would read it with more maturity and understanding. But I also think something else was at work: I found that knowing all the possibilities was not enough. I closed the book still needing help in weaving it all into a whole. Now that you are nearing the end of our twenty-one-day adventure, you may feel similar trepidations: *How do I put it all together?* You have tried a number of richly varied ways to spend time with God. But it's time for more than familiarizing yourself with options. You want to establish some regularity. You want to continue to use different ways and means, but you need a pattern that provides some comfort and regularity.

Here are some pointers.

## DON'T WORRY AS MUCH ABOUT THE WHAT AS THE WHETHER

It matters far more *that* you pray than that you put every quiet time together perfectly. The way to learn to pray and the way to continue to pray is simple: You pray. You come to your time and say, "God, here I am." And then you begin, whether with praise and thanks or confession, whether with Bible reading or a nature walk. Maybe you will be eager with anticipation. Perhaps you will be stifling a yawn. The important thing is to do it. You sit your soul down and stay a while. If during some quiet times you do little more than "show up," then let your presence, wandering mind and all, be your offering to God. Perhaps you will not feel much "quiet" within. But the being there is prayer, even if you feel less than calm and collected.

## KEEP ON KEEPING ON WHEN PRAYING GETS DIFFICULT

Prayer can sometimes be like a desert:

As the deer pants for streams of water,
    so my soul pants for you, O God.
My soul thirsts for God, for the living God.
    When can I go and meet with God?
My tears have been my food
    day and night,
while men say to me all day long,
    "Where is your God?"
(Ps. 42:1–3)

You try to pray but everything seems dry. God seems far away. Bible reading doesn't spark life-giving insights. You are left without much feeling or expectancy. You wonder if anyone really hears.

Not only is such an experience normal, but such a "dark night of the soul" can also be a sign of deepening faith. It means you are letting go of old, perhaps distorted, ways of perceiving God. The superficial pictures of God are giving way to more profound images. Your letting go of the familiar creates discomfort. God may be helping you make room for a deeper, more enduring pattern of prayer. But while a more profound approach is taking root, the sensation is one of lack. We are saying good-bye to the old to greet the new.

It helps to remember on such days that even dry times can be lifted up to God in faith. You keep in mind that, as contemplative writer Thomas Merton explains, "There is no such thing as a prayer in which 'nothing is done' or 'nothing happens,' although there may well be a prayer in which nothing is perceived or felt or thought."[1]

Perhaps you need simply to stay with things a moment longer. Athletes in training know that they will frequently hit a place where everything in them screams, "Quit!" But they tell themselves, "Just another lap, just another block, just another round." Soon they are back in the flow. They can go on.

Whatever your dulled feelings, then, you continue in faith, knowing that the person who trusts in God will eventually "be like a tree planted by the water that sends out its roots by the stream. It does not fear when heat comes;. . . It has no worries in a year of drought" (Jeremiah 17:8). So while you cannot always feel spiritually enthusiastic (life is not that way), you can pray, in spite of flagging emotion. You keep going, believing that God will reward you with the gift of his presence.

## MAKE PRAYER A BIG ENOUGH PRIORITY THAT YOU PLAN IT INTO YOUR DAILY LIFE, EVEN WHEN IT'S NOT EASY

Some things in life seem to happen naturally, effortlessly. But most things happen because we deem them important enough to ensure that they happen. No matter how busy, few of us neglect to eat, sleep, show up on time at work. We know we must, so we *do*. We hardly question it.

Quiet times with God deserve similar significance. Bursts of inspiration refresh us, but they go only so far. We also enlist the will. For truly big projects, of which building a life of prayer is one, you cannot do without deliberateness.

You will have to confront some questions, then: Will you seek God's face whether you feel in fine form or not? Will prayer serve as the lifeblood of your existence, not merely an add-on when convenient (or when you're desperate)? Will you seek first the kingdom of God? Such questions go to the heart (and soul) of the matter.

This means taking stock. "I'm often a member," writes Willow Creek pastor Bill Hybels, "of the club whose motto is 'When all else fails, pray.' Why pray when I can worry? Why pray when I can work myself to death trying to get what I need without help? Why pray when I can go without?"[2] At the root of our prayerlessness is often an unwillingness to depend on God in everything. We think we can wing it, at least in some areas. The result is that too often we fail to plan to pray. And so we fail. Until, that is, things fall apart and our myth of self-sufficiency gets punctured.

There's another way. Fix your will on the reality that God calls you to pray. Decide to do more than squeeze devotional times in around the edges. Give God more than emotional leftovers. Make times with God—however creatively you devise them—a matter of careful design. Take to heart Paul's injunction to "pray continually" (1 Thess. 5:17). Time with God is not an interruption to the life we live. It is its source.

The answer to how to establish a regular time with God, then, has to do with more than your Day-Timer or wall calendar. It has to do with your resolve and your desire. Should you pray an hour a day? Perhaps. God may be calling you to more. But God may also want you to care less about keeping an eye on your watch and more about simply deciding to become a man or woman of prayer. With the big picture settled, with the allegiance declared, the details tend to work themselves out.

My friend Darrell was telling me of his renewed efforts to pray more. One morning something came up and he had to rush out the door. "Here I was in the shower," he told me, "getting ready and feeling guilty for not spending time with God." But then I felt God say to me, 'Why not *now*?' I did not have my regular time with him, but I could use the moments I had right where I was. And so I prayed my way through the shower!" God helped Darrell along. He brought a well-timed reminder and a grace-filled alternative.

Perhaps a job that requires you to work at dawn makes it impractical for you to pray every morning. Your boss won't let you slow down. Perhaps your toddlers' erratic sleep patterns rouse you and confound your best intentions. You can't even count on their taking regular afternoon naps. The answer is not to give up but to become more creative. And to remember your call and your resolve. I know one woman whose young children kept her constantly occupied. "But," she told me with a twinkle in her eye, "I play hide-and-seek with them every day. While they are hiding, I pull out my Bible. It gives me just a few moments for devotions. But it's something." I know executives who spend at least some of their lunch hour walking around the grounds of their corporate headquarters so they can be alone with God. For you the solution may look different. But God is sure to come along to help you.

And if your schedule seems impossible, pray about it. Perhaps God has an answer for the long haul that you don't see right now: A job change, a new assignment at the office, a downsizing of your volunteer commitments. As you pray, as your love for God grows, as you see your quiet times with God transforming your life, things will come out right. You might even be led to change your financial commitments, simplifying your schedule and your lifestyle to ensure more time for the things of God.

Through it all don't forget that prayer, even here in the mapping out of your devotional life—especially here—cannot be dispensed with. Bathe your planning in a desire for God's purposes to rule. Ask God in to make things new. Allow God to take your plans and multiply their good effects.

---

Try this: Spend time praising God for his goodness, for his plans for you, for his ability to do what he promises. Confess that you have been fickle in your commitments to pray. Enlist him now in your plans for quiet times ahead. Take a sheet of paper and list every obstacle to your spending the time that he deserves—and your soul requires. Lift them up to God. Begin asking for guidance: When should you have quiet times? For how long at a time? Write down your plan, tentative though it may be. Then move on to your regular prayer concerns and Bible reading.

## LESSON OF THE DAY

*Don't fail to plan.*

# Continue to Grow

*God can be trusted to bring to completion
what he has begun in you.*

I have kept a journal since I was in my early twenties. Sometimes I enjoy pulling an old volume off the shelf and flipping through and reading of struggles I had forgotten or incidents I only dimly remember. Years may separate me from the jottings, but I am often struck by a common theme, a recurring pattern, a current relevance. I no longer write of crying babies disturbing my sleep (my children are older now). I don't record the struggles of a young pastor getting his start (I haven't pastored a church for years). The family finances are not as precarious. But the repeated lessons—learning to trust God with my career, struggling to be a better parent, becoming a faithful prayer—these I learn and relearn. I am far from finished. Over and over and at deeper and deeper levels I see who I am and what I must do.

Do you sometimes feel that the big lessons will take you a lifetime to master? That God must have a great fund of forbearance when you require repeated tries to get them right? If you are like most people I know, the truths that matter most will have to work themselves into you again and again in ever more profound ways.

I suspect you will find it so with cultivating a better quiet time with God. Whatever progress you have made over these last days, I commend to you two qualities that will help you stay on a growing edge for the *next* twenty-one days and, God willing, for the days and months and years beyond.

## PATIENCE

Our culture conditions us to expect the instantaneous. We want microwave convenience even in matters of the soul. We have become, as writer Sue Monk Kidd once wrote, "quickaholics." So we get tough on ourselves when old habits do not immediately give way to new. We feel frustrated.

The Bible, however, speaks often of patience. Paul the apostle spoke of our "being strengthened with all power according to [God's] glorious might so that you may have great endurance and patience" (Col. 1:11). Of course, the reality of our life with God is an accomplished fact (through Christ's once-for-all sacrifice), but it is also a present process and a future reality. This is why Paul told the church at Philippi, "my dear friends, as you have always obeyed . . . continue to work out your salvation with fear and trembling, for it is God who works in you to will and to act according to his good purpose" (Phil. 2:12–13). The idea is not that we work *off* our standing with God; no, we enjoy access and intimacy with God by grace, through forgiving love. But we *do* keep at it, we work out to the finish all the glorious implications. You and I don't earn salvation, but we still learn, throughout all of life, what it means to live as saved men and women. We take a lifetime to plumb the depths and heights of prayer. That takes an active and sustained and ongoing willingness on our part. It takes perseverance. It takes patience.

The nineteenth-century missionary pioneer William Carey once wrote to a friend, "If after my removal anyone should think it worth his while to write my life, I will give you a criterion by which you may judge of its correctness. If he give me credit for being a plodder he will describe me justly.... I can plod. That is my only genius. I can persevere in any definite pursuit. To this I owe everything."[1]

More important than having it said of you that your devotions sparked awakenings, that your prayers moved continents, that your faith awed associates, will be that you tried, that you kept at your quiet times, that you steadily grew in grace.

## EXPECTANCY

Patience does not live off itself. It does not thrive alone. To continue, you will need one indispensable virtue: hope.

I refer to a particular kind of hope. This is no vague tendency gracing those with naturally sunny dispositions. This is not mere optimism. I am not talking about self-confidence. No, hope that keeps you going and growing has to do with *God*-confidence. You will need an expectancy based in nothing less than God himself. This is what sustained Paul's hope for the believers at Philippi. He wrote of "being confident of this, that he [God] who began a good work in you will carry it on to completion until the day of Christ Jesus" (Phil. 1:6). Ultimately it is not our wisdom or persistence or niceness. It is his patience with *us* that ultimately allows us to become more than we've been.

That can fuel your determination to keep going. When the finish line comes in view, the distance runner inevitably gains a burst of energy. For someone like you and me, trying to become more faithful and devoted, knowing that God is in it and with us makes all the difference. We come to know our efforts are not futile.

The contemplative monk and writer Thomas Merton once wrote of his irritation with his faults. But then, he reflected, "It seems to me the most absurd thing in the world is to be upset because I am weak and distracted and blind and constantly make mistakes! What else do I expect? Does God love me any less because I can't make myself a saint by my own power and in my own way? He loves me more because I am so clumsy and helpless without Him—and underneath what I am He sees me as I will one day be by His pure gift. . . . [T]hat pleases Him—and therefore it pleases me and I attend to His great love which is my joy."[2] Merton rediscovered grace. He realized that God would love and help.

Over the past weeks, working on these chapters, I have seen my quiet times with God grow. I have felt more drawn to spend time with God. God has helped me maintain more semblance of regularity. After years of studying the great spiritual classics, after countless hopes and prayers that I become a more faithful prayer, I see incremental changes. I still awake some mornings and muster little better than a groggy, reluctant greeting to God. I still occasionally oversleep and rush out the door with mostly hurried prayers for help.

But I believe that God will keep working with me. I believe that he won't give up on you, either.

Be patient. Have hope. No need to give up when the best is yet to come.

---

Try this: Take time now to reflect with God on these last twenty-one days. Write down a couple of the most significant discoveries. Ask God to continue to "work in" what you are learning. Now jot down obstacles that still dog your efforts to pray and seek God. Lift them up in prayer to God, asking for the help that only he can give. Take your time! Then pray this prayer:

Lord, I acknowledge that you have begun a good work in me. I thank you that you can be trusted to carry it on to completion to the end of my life, to the end of time. Help me now, in the days and weeks to come, truly to live for you. I want to experience the grace and power that you offer through Jesus. In his name and through the Holy Spirit's power, Amen.

## LESSON OF THE DAY

*God can be trusted to bring to completion what he has begun in you.*

# NOTES

## DAY 1: Start Simply

1. Richard Foster, *Celebration of Discipline,* rev. ed. (San Francisco: Harper & Row, 1988), 2.

## DAY 2: Approach God Confidently

1. Julian of Norwich, *Clothed in Love,* Upper Room Spiritual Classics (Nashville: Upper Room Books, 1997), 7.

## DAY 3: Establish a Balanced Devotional Diet

1. C. S. Lewis, *Mere Christianity* (New York: Collier/Macmillan, 1952), 169.
2. Steve Brown, *Approaching God* (Nashville: Moorings, 1996), 18.

## DAY 4: Read Scripture for All It's Worth (Part 1)

1. Tilden Edwards, *Living in the Presence* (San Francisco: Harper & Row, 1987), 93.
2. Martin L. Smith, *The Word Is Very Near You* (Cambridge, Mass.: Cowley, 1989), 129.
3. Dietrich Bonhoeffer, *Life Together* (New York: Harper & Row, 1954), 82.
4. Note on John 15:1, *The NIV Study Bible* (Grand Rapids: Zondervan, 1985), 1626.
5. Macrina Wiederkehr, *A Tree Full of Angels* (San Francisco: HarperSanFrancisco, 1988), 51.

## DAY 5: Read Scripture for All It's Worth (Part 2)

1. Dom Marmion, *Union with God,* trans. Mother Mary St. Thomas (St. Louis: B. Herder, 1949), 184, quoted in Wiederkehr, *A Tree Full of Angels,* 52.
2. Robert Mulholland, "Spiritual Reading of Scripture," *Weavings* (November/December 1988): 31.
3. Wiederkehr, *A Tree Full of Angels,* 56–57.
4. Martin L. Smith, *The Word Is Very Near You* (Cambridge, Mass.: Cowley, 1989), 135.

### DAY 6: Pray the Promises

1. Dietrich Bonhoeffer, *Psalms: The Prayer Book of the Bible* (Minneapolis: Augsburg, 1970), 11.

2. Peter Kreeft, *Prayer: The Great Conversation* (San Francisco: Ignatius, 1991), 101.

3. Armin Gusswein, "Armin Gusswein's School of Prayer," published by International Intercessors/A Ministry of World Vision International, no date, 1.

### DAY 7: Make Friends with Silence

1. Cornelius Plantinga, "Background Noise," *Christianity Today* (July 17, 1995): 42.

2. Henri J. M. Nouwen, *The Way of the Heart* (San Francisco: HarperSanFrancisco, 1981), 52–53.

3. Thomas Kelly, *Testament of Devotion* (New York: Harper & Row, 1941), 38–39.

### DAY 8: Listen to God's Still, Small Voice

1. Bill Hybels, *Too Busy Not to Pray* (Downers Grove, Ill.: InterVarsity Press, 1988), 108-09.

2. Diane Eble, *Knowing the Voice of God* (Grand Rapids: Zondervan, 1996), 121.

3. Dallas Willard, *In Search of Guidance* (San Francisco: HarperSanFrancisco, 1993), 21.

### DAY 9: Devote a Quiet Time to the Lord's Prayer

1. John Cassian, *Making Life a Prayer,* Upper Room Spiritual Classics (Nashville: Upper Room, 1997), 52.

### DAY 10: Experiment with a Journal

1. Frederick Buechner, *Listening to Your Life* (San Francisco: HarperSanFrancisco, 1992), 127.

2. Gordon MacDonald, *Ordering Your Private World* (Nashville: Thomas Nelson, 1985), 131.

### DAY 11: Let Others' Prayers Jump-Start Yours

1. *The Book of Common Prayer* (New York: Seabury, 1979), 234.

2. Ibid., 832–33.

3. Francis of Assisi, quoted in Roger Pooley and Philip Seddon, *The Lord of the Journey* (London: Collins, 1986), 36–37.

4. A. W. Tozer, *The Knowledge of the Holy* (New York: Harper & Row, 1961), quoted in Bob Benson, Sr., and Michael W. Benson, *Disciplines for the Inner Life* (Nashville: Thomas Nelson, 1989), 24.

5. Susanna Wesley, quoted in *Prayers Across the Centuries* (Wheaton, Ill.: Harold Shaw, 1993), 107.

6. Thérèse of Lisieux, quoted in *Prayers Across the Centuries,* 125.

## DAY 12: Find a Friend

1. Thomas à Kempis, *The Imitation of Christ,* I.4.

## DAY 14: Invite a Child into Your Devotional Time

1. Quoted in Mary Batchelor, ed., *The Lion Prayer Collection* (Oxford, England: Lion, 1992), 306.

2. Betty Shannon Cloyd, *Children and Prayer* (Nashville: Upper Room, 1997), 102.

3. Ibid., 21.

## DAY 15: Dip into the Devotional Classics

1. Jean-Pierre de Caussade, *The Sacrament of the Present Moment,* trans. Kitty Muggeridge (San Francisco: Harper & Row, 1989), 3.

2. Augustine, *Confessions,* Book 1, chapter 1, author's translation.

3. Ibid., Book 10, chapter 27.

4. Julian of Norwich, *Encountering God's Love,* Upper Room Spiritual Classics, Series 2 (Nashville: Upper Room Books, 1998).

5. Brother Lawrence, *The Practice of the Presence of God,* trans. John J. Delaney (New York: Doubleday, 1977), 101.

6. Oswald Chambers, *My Utmost for His Highest* (Uhrichsville, Ohio: Barbour, 1963), 210.

7. Ibid., 217.

8. Samuel Johnson quoted in *Prayers Across the Centuries* (Wheaton, Ill.: Harold Shaw, 1993), 107.

## DAY 16: Pray Your Way Through the Psalms (Part 1)

1. Dietrich Bonhoeffer, *Psalms: The Prayer Book of the Bible* (Minneapolis: Augsburg, 1970), 25.

2. Eugene Peterson, *Answering God* (San Francisco: Harper & Row, 1989), 3–4.

## DAY 17: Pray Your Way Through the Psalms (Part 2)

1. Athanasius, *Ad Marcellinum,* quoted in James Luther Mays, *Psalms* (Louisville, Ky.: Westminster/John Knox, 1994), 1, cited in Larry R. Kalajainen, *Psalms for the Journey* (Nashville: Upper Room Books, 1996), 10.

## DAY 19: Experiment with Varied Approaches

1. Eugene Peterson, *The Contemplative Pastor* (Dallas: Word, 1989), 78.
2. John Calvin, *Institutes,* I.5.1.

## DAY 20: Lay Out a Realistic Plan

1. Thomas Merton: *Thoughts in Solitude* (Boston: Shambhala, 1956), 46.

2. Bill Hybels, *Too Busy Not to Pray* (Downers Grove, Ill.: InterVarsity Press, 1988), 88.

## DAY 21: Continue to Grow

1. William Carey, quoted in Roger Pooley and Philip Seddon, *The Lord of the Journey* (London: Collins, 1986), 281.

2. Thomas Merton, *The Sign of Jonas* (San Diego: Harcourt Brace, 1953), 102–103.